Did Jesus
REALLY
Say?

Did Jesus REALLY Say?

EXAMINING A SCHOLARLY THREAT
TO THE GOSPELS

—————— Don Green ——————

Did Jesus Really Say?
Examining a Scholarly Threat to the Gospels

Don Green

Copyright © 2023 Donald Green

Second printing 2024

ISBN: 978-0-9987156-2-9

Cover design and typeset by www.greatwriting.org

Printed in the United States of America

Trust the Word Press
575 Chamber Drive
Milford, OH 45150

**TRUST THE WORD
PRESS**
BIBLICAL THINKING FOR BIBLICAL LIVING

Contents

To Him who alone has the words of eternal life

(John 6:68)

Preface

"The words that I have spoken to you are spirit and are life" (John 6:63).

That statement from our blessed Lord (and other statements like it) informs the high value that any reverent student of Scripture should place on the record of His life and words found in the four canonical Gospels. The biblical record gives us the only infallible account of the teaching ministry of Christ.

The infinite value of His teaching places a responsibility on pastors and teachers to protect the integrity of the scriptural record. After all, we have an adversary, the devil, who "prowls about like a roaring lion, seeking someone to devour" (1 Peter 5:8). What better way to destroy souls than to undermine confidence in the self-revelatory teaching ministry of our Lord?

Indeed, from the beginning of time, the strategy of Satan has been to cast doubt on the reliability of the Word of God. The fall of man can be traced to the insidious question the serpent posed to Eve: "Did God actually say . . .?" (Gen. 3:1; ESV).

Knowledge of the devil's schemes should cause every true believer to guard against any philosophy or interpretive scheme that casts even a shadow of suspicion upon the veracity of what God has said in the Bible.

That's why I am publishing this book.

I want to warn and protect earnest Christians—especially men who are preparing for ministry—from a form of *evangelical* scholarship that explicitly casts doubt on the recorded words of Jesus. These philosophies lead the student, not to read, heed, and trust the words of our Lord, but to sit in speculative judgment of whether He ever said such things in the first place.

Instead of words that are "spirit and life," these scholars leave us with sayings which Christ may or may not have spoken at all. Such academic speculations threaten the integrity of the Gospels, leaving the student repeatedly asking the question, "Did Jesus *really* say what the Bible says He did?"

Such doubt and skepticism are not produced by the wisdom that comes down from above.

Nevertheless, these professors do have an appearance of wisdom—so much so, that they would intimidate the uninitiated into silence. They use unfamiliar interpretative categories and quote obscure ancient historians. In so doing, they attempt to impose presuppositions by which they insist the gospels—and thus the words of Jesus—must be interpreted. Few seminary students, and even fewer "ordinary" Christians, have the time, resources, or background to evaluate—let alone discern—such views and assertions.

Theologically, these views lead inexorably to a full-blown denial of the inerrancy and infallibility of Scripture—even if their current proponents deny that intention or foresee that result.

Pastorally, these speculative theories will devastate the long-term power and confidence of local church ministry. What professors whisper in their classrooms or tuck away on their website today, their students will shout from their pulpits tomorrow. If the *teachers* question the words of Jesus, what will become of their *students*?

All that said, this book requires some explanation. I first wrote this material over twenty years ago as the thesis for my

Master of Theology degree. A brief synopsis was soon published as an article in the Spring 2001 edition of *The Master's Seminary Journal*.[1]

Providentially, my life as a pastor does not—at least for now—allow me to bring the material up to date by interacting with subsequent debate. The resultant "time warp" factor is not perfect—especially since I occasionally have seen others quote my article over the years.

I happily acknowledge that limitation up front. It is not ideal. But a scholarly ideal need not, in my opinion, stifle the publication of research that might help the body of Christ.

The fact that this work may not be *current* does not mean that it is *inaccurate*. The content of this book simply stands as if it had been published in 2001. The principles I defend in this book transcend the evolving speculations of modern scholarship.

Scholars are sometimes thin-skinned, so a word of clarification is also probably wise. I am making no statement, positive or negative, about *other* views held by the men I critique. I offer no final judgments about their orthodoxy. My focus is limited solely to the issue at hand.

At the same time, I do not apologize for stating that this book addresses a crucial error that, taken to its logical conclusions, would ultimately deny the authority of Scripture. The theories these men follow enshroud the teaching of Christ in a rolling fog and hide Him from modern readers of the Gospels. Whether these men *intend* that outcome or not is completely beside the point.

The late Dr. Robert Thomas had primary responsibility for the academic oversight of my thesis. He was a noble man of rigorous scholarship, integrity, and Christian virtue. I deeply thank God for his academic and spiritual influence on my life, even though I now see some theological issues (unrelated to the content of this book) in a way that my now-glorified professor probably would have hesitated to endorse while on earth.

---

1 That article was subjected to a demonstrably misleading review in the October – December 2001 issue of *Bibliotheca Sacra*.

I acknowledge my friend Jim Holmes for his editorial assistance and creative contributions to this book. My faithful and remarkable daughter Hannah has been a gift from God to me in the many administrative tasks necessary to support my venture into publications.

I especially want to thank my wife, Nancy, for her unfailing support through the many years of study and ministry that have made this book possible. You certainly would not have this work in your hands apart from the faithful love, influence, and support she has given to me and our family over the past thirty-five years.

May God use this book greatly to His glory.

Don Green
May 2023
Cincinnati, Ohio

1

Introduction

The Need for this Study
....

In recent years, evangelical New Testament scholarship has been debating whether the canonical Gospels contain the exact words of Jesus (*ipsissima verba,* the "very words") or only summaries of His teaching (*ipsissima vox,* the "very voice"). Some writers are increasingly embracing a view of *ipsissima vox* in the Gospels that gives broad latitude to the Gospel writers to edit the words of Jesus and even create words to put on His lips. Proponents of this view assert that this practice is not misleading, because the Gospel writers are relaying the intended meaning of Jesus' teaching, even if He never said the words Himself.

These assertions demand closer attention, particularly in light of the orthodox doctrine of the verbal inspiration of the Scriptures. Inspiration refers to "a supernatural, providential influence of God's Holy Spirit upon the human authors which caused them to write what He wished to be written for the communication of revealed truth to others."[2] Because God is

2   J. I. Packer, *"Fundamentalism" and the Word of God* (Grand Rapids: Eerdmans, 1958), 77.

a God of truth, inspiration guarantees both factual accuracy and verbal precision in the Bible, a position that is verified by the prophetic, historical, and grammatical detail in the Bible. Inspiration must therefore be accounted for in interpretation.

In the 1980's, New Testament scholars seemed to agree that verbally precise quotations of Jesus were not necessary to uphold the traditional doctrine of inspiration. These scholars often asserted that the Gospel writers took greater freedom in recording His words than modern standards that employ quotation marks would allow. Under this view, the greater leeway is not contrary to the inspiration or inerrancy of Scripture because the Gospel writers never intended to follow today's linguistic conventions. The treatment of these issues was brief among these writers.[3] They did not address significant issues of historiography and scriptural phenomena.

In the 1990's, evangelical writers tried to put the *ipsissima vox* position on more substantial analytical ground. They made arguments based on ancient history and offered scriptural examples in support of their position. They asserted that the Gospel writers could modify Jesus' words without violating the principle of factual accuracy because the alleged changes themselves were the product of the Spirit's work of inspiration.[4]

In support, they claim that the standard of secular historical reporting of the time allowed historians to summarize and modify reported speeches to record the general sense, not the precise words, of the speaker. in other words, the literary

3   Paul D. Feinberg, "The Meaning of Inerrancy," in *Inerrancy*, ed. Norman L. Geisler (Grand Rapids: Zondervan, 1980), 301 (one paragraph); Robert L. Stein, *The Synoptic Problem* (Grand Rapids: Baker, 1987), 156 (one paragraph); Roger Nicole, "The Nature of Inerrancy," in *Inerrancy and Common Sense*, ed. Roger R. Nicole and J. Ramsey Michaels (Grand Rapids: Baker, 1980), 84-85 (one paragraph).

4   Darrell L. Bock, "The Words of Jesus in the Gospels: Live, Jive, or Memorex," in *Jesus Under Fire*, ed. Michael J. Wilkins and J. P. Moreland (Grand Rapids: Zondervan, 1995), 73-99; Daniel B. Wallace, "An *Apologia* for a Broad View of *Ipsissima Vox*," paper presented to the 51st Annual Meeting of the Evangelical Theological Society (Danvers, Mass: November, 1999).

context of the first century would have conditioned the Gospel writers toward a more relaxed standard in presenting and editing the words of Jesus. Further, parallel accounts of the Gospels allegedly show verbal discrepancies that can only be explained by editorial activity among the Gospel writers.

Crucially, some *ipsissima vox* proponents go even further to distance themselves from the doctrine of inspiration in this context. They say that inspiration should be set aside and that the Bible should be "treated like any other book" by subjecting it to the same critical methodology applied to other documents from ancient history. Human procedure, rather than divine inspiration, becomes the governing presupposition in interpretation.[5]

Other scholars have challenged the *ipsissima vox* view stated above. They warn that it threatens inerrancy because it dehistoricizes Jesus' words in the Gospels. As these men see it, the doctrine of inspiration requires either a more restricted view of *ipsissima vox*[6] or a working presumption that the Gospels consistently record the *ipsissima verba* of Christ.[7] The debate has spilled over to the pages of the *Journal of the Evangelical Theological Society* as part of a broader debate over the role of historical criticism in the interpretation of the Gospels.[8]

5   Their willingness to set aside the presupposition of inspiration installs the interpreter as the judge of Scripture, rather than Scripture as the judge of the interpreter. Devout students of the Bible should let that sink in deeply as they consider these issues for themselves.

6 Bob Wilkin, "Toward a Narrow View of *Ipsissima Vox*," paper presented to the 52nd Annual Meeting of the Evangelical Theological Society (Nashville, Tenn: November 2000).

7   Robert L. Thomas, "Impact of Historical Criticism on Theology and Apologetics," in *The Jesus Crisis*, ed. Robert L. Thomas and F. David Farnell (Grand Rapids: Kregel, 1998), 367-374.

8   See Grant R. Osborne, "Historical Criticism and the Evangelical," *Journal of the Evangelical Theological Society* 42 (June 1999): 202-204; Robert L. Thomas, "Historical Criticism and the Evangelical: Another View," *Journal of the Evangelical Theological Society* 43 (March 2000): 106-107; cf. Osborne, "Historical Criticism: A Brief Response to Robert Thomas's 'Other View,'" *Journal of the Evangelical Theological Society* 43 (March 2000): 113-117.

Given this ongoing controversy in evangelical New Testament scholarship, as well as its potential impact on evangelical confidence in the historical accuracy of the Gospels, the present study is both timely and necessary.

Method of the Study

This book will examine modern statements of *ipsissima vox* in light of an orthodox view of the doctrine of inspiration. To accomplish this goal, I will first examine the doctrine of inspiration along with some of its implications for the precision of the words of Scriptures. Differing understandings of those implications will be considered and evaluated.

After inspiration has been discussed, the book will address broader issues pertaining to the interpretation of the Gospels. The relatively new field of genre analysis will be considered, along with the different ways it has been used to interpret the Gospels. The nature of the Gospels will be contrasted with the classifications that have been offered to date.

This discussion will establish the general background that is influencing modern scholarship. We will see that genre analysis to date has been marked by conflicting definitions and conclusions. It also neglects the unique inspiration of the Gospels. As a result, it is not a reliable tool to use in biblical interpretation.

We will then turn attention to the nature of ancient historiography, which provides much of the basis for modern formulations of the *ipsissima vox* position. How did secular historians who lived at and prior to the time of the writing of the Gospels approach their task? Evangelical use of that historical data will then be assessed in light of the doctrine of inspiration, including the power of the Holy Spirit to enable the Gospel writers to record the words of Jesus with greater precision than secular historians could achieve as they wrote on secular subjects.

We will then assess the scriptural arguments advanced in favor of *ipsissima vox*. How do we understand the scriptural data in which the Gospel writers seem to vary in their record of words and deeds rooted in the same occasion in Jesus' life? The explanations offered by *ipsissima vox* proponents will be stated and evaluated. We will see that their examples do not support their conclusions, and a better explanation exists that trustworthy scholars have accepted for many years.

Following that analysis, I will summarize this research, draw conclusions that uphold confidence in the biblical record, and offer suggestions for further study.

Limitations of the Study

This book is targeted for Christians and students who already profess a belief in the verbal inspiration of Scriptures. The writer assumes that his readers are generally sympathetic to that doctrine and are further familiar with the scriptural arguments that have traditionally been used to support it. Consequently, the following pages devote little space to defending the doctrine or stating the grounds in support of it. The purpose here is to work out the implications of inspiration in the context of the *ipsissima vox* discussion, not deal with inspiration *per se*.

A study of this type touches many areas of New Testament scholarship on the Gospels. The narrow focus of this book will prevent me from interacting with other issues that are necessary to be abreast of current Gospel study. Detailed interaction with the nature of historical criticism will not be attempted here, although I recognize that it underlies most current literature on the Gospels. Further, since this book is directed toward evangelicals, interaction with the liberal methods or conclusions of The Jesus Seminar has been intentionally excluded.[9]

Similarly, a discussion of the standard arguments advanced in favor of Markan priority and literary dependence cannot be undertaken at this time, although the effects of literary depen-

---

9   The fruit of the Jesus Seminar is found in Robert W. Funk, Roy W. Hoover, and the Jesus Seminar, *The Five Gospels: The Search for the Authentic Words of Jesus* (New York: Macmillan, 1993).

dence on the *ipsissima vox* discussion will be addressed toward the end of the book.

Further, this book is limited to an evaluation of the arguments in favor of *ipsissima vox* that its advocates have discussed at length—particularly the historical and scriptural positions that undergird their writings. That means the important issue of whether Jesus primarily spoke Aramaic or Greek will not be addressed in this paper. [10]

Similarly, this paper will not address the use of the Old Testament by the New Testament writers. Does the manner in which the New Testament writers use the Old Testament provide a useful analogy to the way the Gospel writers may have recorded the words of Jesus?[11] That pertinent question also lies outside the scope of this study. All these areas have been avoided for the sake of an in-depth analysis of current evangelical literature on *ipsissima vox*, and attention is now turned to that topic.

---

10   If Jesus spoke in Aramaic, there arguably would have been an inevitable, even if slight, linguistic entropy in translating the spoken Aramaic of Jesus into the written Greek of the Gospels. The long-held scholarly opinion is that Jesus spoke and taught primarily in Aramaic, a view represented, for example, in Joseph A. Fitzmyer, "The Languages of Palestine in the First Century A.D.," *Catholic Biblical Quarterly* 32 (October 1970): 501-531. However, more recent writers have challenged that presumption and support the view that Jesus not only spoke but also taught in Greek at various times during His ministry. See Stanley E. Porter, "Did Jesus Ever Teach in Greek?," *Tyndale Bulletin* 44.2 (November 1993): 199-235; cf. Wallace, "An *Apologia*," 6; and Wallace, *Greek Grammar Beyond the Basics* (Grand Rapids: Zondervan, 1996), 17-18.

11   Bock states, "Numerous New Testament citations of the Old are not word for word, even after taking into account translation from Hebrew into Greek [citations omitted]. If the Bible can summarize a citation of itself in this way, then to see the same technique in its handling the words of Jesus should come as no surprise" (Bock, "The Words of Jesus," 78.) Thomas, however, distinguishes between New Testament citations of the Old, where the Old Testament was available for comparison to evaluate differences, and the Gospels' record of Jesus' words where no other authoritative written source of Jesus' words was available. Readers were dependent on the Gospel writers' report because they had no other standard to evaluate the accuracy of the reporting (Thomas, "Impact of Historical Criticism on Theology and Apologetics," 368).

2

Inspiration and Its Implications

This chapter will establish a theological framework for evaluating the *ipsissima vox* position. The doctrine of the verbal inspiration of Scripture will be briefly considered. After the doctrine is stated, its implications for the words of Scripture in general will be evaluated. Those implications will then be illustrated through prophetic, historical, and grammatical features in the Scriptures. Then potential objections to these implications of inspiration will be set forth with a response. A summary and conclusions will then follow.

An Overview of Inspiration

The doctrine of inspiration is based in part on 2 Timothy 3:16, which says, "All Scripture is inspired by God and profitable for teaching, for reproof, for correction, for training in righteousness." The phrase "inspired by God" comes from the Greek term θεόπνευστος, which means "God-breathed."

It carries the sense that God breathed out the Scriptures or, stated differently, that God spoke in written form through the Scriptures.[12]

Another key passage in support of the doctrine is 2 Peter 1:20-21, which reads, "But know this first of all, that no prophecy of Scripture is a matter of one's own interpretation, for no prophecy was ever made by an act of human will, but men moved by the Holy Spirit spoke from God."

As stated earlier, J. I. Packer defines inspiration as "a supernatural, providential influence of God's Holy Spirit upon the human authors that caused them to write what He wished to be written for the communication of revealed truth to others."[13] While that definition suffices for present purposes, evangelicals have set forth many potential definitions of inspiration with varying degrees of nuance.[14]

The doctrine of inspiration means that the Bible is entirely from God. Human error is not mixed into its production. R. Laird Harris writes:

> God superintended the very choice of words in the Holy Volume so that it may be truly said to be entirely God's Word without admixture of human error. This may also be expressed by insisting that the Bible is "true throughout" or by specifying that it is without error in "fact, doctrine, or judgment."[15]

In recent times, some evangelicals have moved away from that definition, restricting the Bible's authority to areas of "faith and practice," but not its absolute truthfulness in every

12   Wayne A. Grudem, "Scripture's Self-Attestation and the Problem of Formulating a Doctrine of Scripture," in *Scripture and Truth*, ed. D. A. Carson and John D. Woodbridge (Grand Rapids: Baker, 1992), 39.

13   Packer, *"Fundamentalism" and the Word of God*, 77.

14   For an evaluation of different formulations of the doctrine of inspiration, see Louis Igou Hodges, "Evangelical Definitions of Inspiration," *Journal of the Evangelical Theological Society* 37 (March 1994): 99-114.

15   R. Laird Harris, *Inspiration and Canonicity of the Scriptures*, rev. and updated ed. (Greenville, SC: A Press, 1995), 11-12.

area. This view excludes inerrancy in areas of history and science.[16]

Implications of Inspiration

A Deductive Approach to Scripture

The doctrine of inspiration has significant implications for the manner in which the interpreter approaches the Scripture. He must realize that he is approaching a living, authoritative Word because it is the Word of God (cf. Heb. 4:12). As such, the reader must know in advance that the Bible is true in all that it affirms, and not exercise his interpretive judgment in a way that assigns error or untruth to the pages of Scripture.

The commitment to the inspiration and inerrancy of Scripture has important methodological implications for the interpreter as he examines the phenomena that the Bible exhibits in individual passages. For example, how should the interpreter assess such matters as the use of the Old Testament in the New, chronological difficulties, or the reconciliation of biblical history with secular sources? Conservatives have long held that the self-referential statements of Scripture must have priority in making those interpretive decisions, so that the truthfulness of the Bible is affirmed in the handling of the data. Difficult passages cannot rightly be used to impute error to the text. Instead, inspiration guarantees that difficult texts can eventually be explained, even if the interpreter cannot resolve the difficulty at the present time.[17]

In other words, the interpreter must adopt a deductive approach to dealing with the Scriptures, one that interprets the Bible from the *starting point* of inspiration. One determines his doctrine of Scripture primarily from the statements

---

16   For a helpful survey, see D. A. Carson, "Recent Developments in the Doctrine of Scripture," in *Hermeneutics, Authority, and Canon*, ed. D. A. Carson and John D. Woodbridge (Grand Rapids: Baker, 1995), 10-20. I reject any such restrictions on inerrancy.

17   Ibid., 23-25.

of Scripture about itself (e.g., Ps. 19:7-9; John 17:17). Because the Bible is true, its details must be interpreted in a manner consistent with its truthfulness. Details not directly bearing on scriptural authority should not undermine or contradict the formulation of a doctrine of Scripture.[18]

Greg Bahnsen puts the question this way: "Does one decide the question of Scriptural inerrancy by an inductive examination of the discursive and individual assertions of Scripture one by one, or by settling on the truth of these special self-referential assertions and then letting them control our approach to all the rest?"[19] In other words, should the interpreter seek to establish inerrancy through an examination of all the individual assertions that the Bible makes, or should he examine all those assertions in light of the Bible's teaching about its own inerrancy?

That question determines how the interpreter will approach the scriptural data. If he suspends his judgment on the truthfulness of the Bible until he has critically examined "all" the evidence, then his *own judgment is the final arbiter of truth*. If, however, the interpreter self-consciously assumes the Bible's truthfulness as he examines the passages under consideration, then the Scripture's self-attestation will be the final arbiter of truth.

Bahnsen insightfully puts it this way: "It is clear to anyone who will reflect seriously on this question that the statements of Scripture *about* Scripture are primary and must determine our attitude toward all the rest."[20]

There are three reasons for this: (1) An exhaustive inductive examination cannot be carried out in practice. (2) By their very character, many scriptural assertions cannot be tested inductively but must be accepted, if at all, on Scripture's own attestation (e.g., Christ's interpretation of His person and work

---

18   J. I. Packer, "Hermeneutics and Biblical Authority," *Themelios* 1 (Autumn 1975): 8.

19   Greg Bahnsen, "Inductivism, Inerrancy, and Presuppositionalism," *Journal of the Evangelical Theological Society* 20 (December 1977): 301.

20   Ibid (emphasis in original).

as being divine and redemptive). (3) Inductive study itself has crucial presuppositions that cannot be accounted for except on a biblical basis, and therefore in a profound sense an inductive study is already committed to the content of these self-referential statements of Scripture.[21]

In words especially pertinent for the present study, Bahnsen writes:

> One cannot but let the Bible speak for itself about its own nature and attributes, and consequently one cannot choose to submit to scriptural truths at some points (e.g., Christ's deity and redeeming work are beyond the adjudication of empirical criticism) and reserve self-sufficient critical authority elsewhere (e.g., historical data are accepted or rejected on the strength of empirical examination).[22]

Bahnsen concludes:

> The question is this: What exercises control over our speculation, evaluation, and conclusions—God's revealed word in Scripture, or some authority external to God's revelation? Do empirical difficulties render the Bible's inerrancy only apparent, or does the Bible's inerrancy render empirical difficulties only apparent? One must begin with the testimony of Scripture to itself, rather than with the allegedly neutral methods of inductivism. And this means acknowledging the veracity of Scripture even when empirical evidence might appear to contradict it (following in the steps of the father of the faithful, Abraham: Rom 4:16-21; Heb 11:17-19).[23]

At the very least, the deductive method means that the interpreter approaches the Scriptures with a deference to the

21 Ibid., 301-302.
22 Ibid., 303.
23 Ibid., 304.

Bible's self-referential truth claims. If he is faced with conflicting interpretive options, one of which affirms the accuracy of the Bible and the other which denies its accuracy, the interpreter gives priority to the truthfulness of the Scripture and chooses the option that does not contradict the Bible's affirmations. This does not relieve the interpreter of the responsibility of facing difficult issues, nor does it answer every difficulty he will face. However, it does provide him with a plumb line to examine his tentative conclusions. A commitment to inspiration allows nothing less.

Verbal Precision in the Scriptures

Necessity of Verbal Precision

Importantly, inspiration also demands a high regard for every single word contained in the text. Every word in the Bible is significant because of its Source. Numerous writers have recognized this factor over the years. Packer, writing on the importance of the *verbal* inspiration of Scripture, says:

> *Words signify and safeguard meaning; the wrong word distorts the intended sense.* Since God inspired the biblical text in order to communicate His Word, it was necessary for him to ensure that the words written were such as did in fact convey it. We do not stress the verbal character of inspiration from a superstitious regard for the original Hebrew and Greek words . . .; we do so from reverent concern for the sense of Scripture. If the words were not wholly God's, then their teaching would not be wholly God's.[24]

Leon Morris writes, "The precise form of words is important."[25] He later adds:

24   Packer, *"Fundamentalism,"* 89-90 (emphasis added).
25   Leon Morris, *I Believe in Revelation* (Grand Rapids: Eerdmans, 1976), 116.

Rational intercourse depends on the use of words. And it is the right use of words that leads us into the inner being of another. Without the right words we are always stumbling. We need not, accordingly, be surprised at the place words occupy in the revelation. They are God's way of making his truth known to his people. [26]

B. B. Warfield also emphasizes the importance of the precise verbal form of the Scriptures when he states, "We come nearer to the meaning of Scripture by the closest attention to the subtleties and minute variations of words and order."[27]

Morris concludes:

> The importance of the words must be stressed. It is only in the measure that we can trust the record that we can apprehend the revelation. If we cannot believe the record we cannot recover the acts of God or the inspired thinking of the writers. We can find only our own ideas about what those acts and that thinking must be. We are dependent on the Bible for the revelation. Apart from the Bible we do not know it.[28]

As the foregoing quotations make clear, the inspiration of Scripture means the interpreter must give high priority to the exact verbal content of the text. All manner of textual detail is scrutinized to assess the bearing it may have on understanding the divine message. A varied verbal form would result in a different meaning.

Having established this traditional position, it now remains to be seen if it will withstand scrutiny of a closer examination of biblical texts.

---

26 Ibid., 118.

27 Benjamin Breckinridge Warfield, *The Inspiration and Authority of the Bible*, ed. Samuel G. Craig with an introduction by Cornelius Van Til (Philadelphia: Presbyterian and Reformed, 1964), 110.

28 Morris, *I Believe in Revelation*, 118.

Evidence of Verbal Precision

Prophetic Detail

One area where the stress on individual words can be evaluated is in the Bible's treatment of prophetic details from the Old Testament that were fulfilled in the life of Christ. Wayne Grudem gives the following illustrative list to show why the interpreter should be unwilling to think of any detail of the Old Testament as "unreliable":[29]

Micah 5:2, Matt. 2:5	He was born in Bethlehem.
Zech. 9:9, John 12:14-15	He rode to Jerusalem on a donkey.
Ps. 41:9, John 13:18	His betrayer ate bread with Him.
Ps. 22:18, John 19:24	Lots were cast for His garments.
Ps. 69:21, John 19:28-30	He was given vinegar to drink.
Ps. 34:20, John 19:36	None of His bones were broken.
Zech. 12:10, John 19:37	He was pierced with a sword.
Isa. 53:9, Matt. 27:57-60	He was buried in a rich man's grave.

That list shows how Scripture focuses on what would seem to be relatively obscure Old Testament details and lifts them to prominence in describing the life of Christ. This is precisely what one would expect from the doctrine of inspiration. If every word is from God, then every word is significant. Thus, the importance and reliability of Scripture goes beyond the enunciation of broad themes. Weight is placed on the details.[30]

Historical Detail

Not only do the Gospel writers draw upon seemingly small details in making the case for fulfilled prophecy, they also demonstrate confidence in the smallest historical details in Old Testament narrative. Grudem illustrates this point by listing 27 different historical points from the Old Testament that

29   Grudem, "Scripture's Self-Attestation," 41.

30   Ibid.

are affirmed as accurate in the New Testament. These details include David's eating of the bread of the Presence (Matt. 12:3-4), the murder of Zechariah between the sanctuary and the altar (Matt. 23:35), Abraham's tithe to Melchizedek (Heb. 7:2), and the words that came from the mouth of Balaam's donkey (2 Peter 2:16). Grudem writes:

> This list indicates a willingness on the part of the New Testament writers to rely on the truthfulness of any part of the historical narratives of the Old Testament. No detail is too insignificant to be used for the instruction of New Testament Christians.[31]

This attention to detail is also illustrated in the manner by Jesus' use of the historical details of the Old Testament. He referred to Abel (Luke 11:51), Noah (Matt. 24:37), Abraham (John 8:56), Sodom (Luke 10:12), Isaac and Jacob (Matt. 8:11), and Jonah (Matt. 12:41), among others. Such references show the confidence He had in the historical reliability of the Old Testament. Again, this is consistent with what one would expect, given the doctrine of inspiration.

Grammatical Detail

As Paul Feinberg has shown, this attention to detail extends to precise grammatical points as well.[32] First, sometimes the entire argument rests on a single word, as when Matthew 22:43-45 uses the word "Lord." Jesus cites Psalm 110:1 and appeals to the use of "Lord" as support for His claim to deity. In John 10:34, 35, Jesus rests his argument on the single word "god" in Psalm 82:6.

Second, at times the entire argument depends on the verb tense used. Jesus uses the present tense of the verb to demonstrate the truth of the resurrection in Matthew 22:32: "I am the

---

31   Ibid., 43.

32   The following discussion is indebted to Paul D. Feinberg, "The Meaning of Inerrancy," in *Inerrancy*, ed. Norman L. Geisler (Grand Rapids: Zondervan, 1980), 286.

God of Abraham, and the God of Isaac, and the God of Jacob. He is not the God of the dead but of the living."

Third, the argument in Galatians 3:16 depends on the singular number "seed" as opposed to the plural "seeds." Feinberg concludes, "Now if the text of Scripture is not inerrant, it is difficult to see the point in these arguments."[33] Also pertinent is Mark 10:45, where the description of Jesus' mission on earth hinges on the difference between the passive and active voice: "For even the Son of Man did not come to be served, but to serve, and to give His life a ransom for many." The Scripture writers often relied on grammatical precision to make their points and showed a concern for detail that is consistent with the expectations of verbal inspiration.[34]

Thus, in their attention to prophetic, historical, and grammatical detail, the New Testament writers demonstrate confidence in the details of the Old Testament, and also demonstrate attention to slight nuances in their own writings. This is what one would expect based on the statements about inspiration and the importance of the verbal form of the Scriptures discussed above.

Necessity of Harmonization

Inspiration also has implications for the way in which the interpreter approaches seemingly divergent statements in the Scriptures. Many evangelical writers have affirmed that a commitment to inspiration requires the interpreter to fit the data into a harmonistic, non-contradictory whole.[35] That conclusion is based on the understanding that the Scriptures are the product of a single divine mind. God will

33   Ibid.

34   This does not imply a duty of the Gospel writers to record full detail at all times. They were free to emphasize the detail necessary to communicate their intended message (cf. John 20:30-31). Details not necessary to the message were omitted with no loss of historical accuracy.

35   E.g., Kelly Osborne, "Impact of Historical Criticism on Gospel Interpretation: A Test Case," in *The Jesus Crisis*, ed. Robert L. Thomas and F. David Farnell (Grand Rapids: Kregel, 1998), 289.

be consistent with Himself, and thus interpretations that lead to internal contradictions in the Scriptures are wrong by definition.[36] Stated differently, if there is a way to understand the passage so that it is in harmony with the rest of Scripture and another way of understanding that conflicts with other Scripture, the former is the correct interpretation.[37] The inspired nature of the documents guarantees that a true harmony exists—even if it is not immediately apparent to the interpreter.[38]

Perspicuity of Scripture

A final implication of inspiration is the doctrine of perspicuity, which holds that the meaning of the Bible is clear. Psalm 19:7 reads, "The testimony of the LORD is sure, making wise the simple." Psalm 119:130 adds, "The unfolding of Your words gives light; it gives understanding to the simple." Wayne Grudem says:

> The "simple" person is not merely one who lacks intellectual ability, but one who lacks sound judgment, who is prone to making mistakes, and who is easily led astray. God's Word is so understandable, so clear, that even this kind of person is made wise by it. This should be a great encouragement to all believers: no believer should think himself or herself too foolish to read Scripture and understand it sufficiently to be made wise by it.[39]

36 Packer, "Hermeneutics and Biblical Authority," 7.

37 Feinberg, "The Meaning of Inerrancy," 297.

38 For further support of the principle of harmonization, see Robert L. Thomas and Stanley N. Gundry, "Is a Harmony of the Gospels Legitimate," in Thomas and Gundry, *A Harmony of the Gospels* (San Francisco: HarperCollins, 1978), 265-268.

39 Wayne Grudem, *Systematic Theology* (Grand Rapids: Zondervan, 1994), 106.

Milton Terry writes:

> It is commonly assumed by the universal sense of mankind that unless one designedly put forth a riddle, he will so speak as to convey his meaning as clearly as possible to others. Hence that meaning of a sentence which most readily suggests itself to a reader or hearer is, in general, to be received as the true meaning, and that alone.[40]

Evangelical Objections to Inspiration Implications

Objections Stated

Despite the foregoing arguments, many evangelicals vigorously object to the notion of letting a presupposition of inspiration and inerrancy influence the interpretation of the biblical phenomena. Daniel Wallace, for example, asserts that we should "treat the Bible like any other book to show that it is *not like* any other book."[41] In other words, the interpreter should ignore the doctrine of inspiration and conduct his investigation by assuming that the Bible is like any other man-made book. Wallace, for one, refuses to let the doctrine of inspiration "govern" his interpretation of the text.[42]

Craig Blomberg similarly sets aside any presupposition of inerrancy in his evaluation of the historical reliability of the Gospels. He writes, "This research has *self-consciously tried to avoid presupposing the infallibility of Scripture or the deity of Christ*, but has merely attempted to follow the standard method

40   Milton Terry, *Biblical Hermeneutics* (Grand Rapids: Zondervan, 1964), 205.

41   Daniel Wallace, "The Synoptic Problem and Inspiration: A Response," July 4, 2000, http://www.bible.org/article/synoptic-problem-and-inspiration-response, accessed 4/24/23.

42   Wallace, "An *Apologia*," 20. In this instance, at least, Wallace would appear to be rejecting a deductive approach to the Scriptures.

of historical enquiry [sic]."[43] Indeed, he criticizes those who would use inspiration as a basis to affirm the historical reliability of the gospels:

> Are the gospels historically reliable? Some conservative readers would reply affirmatively *simply because they believe their doctrine of the inspiration of Scripture requires them to.* This overlooks the fact that God can communicate truth through a wide variety of literary forms; in fact over half of Scripture is written in literary genres other than historical ones—poetry, proverbs, prophecy, epistles, and apocalypses. . . . A superficial appearance of history therefore proves little. . . . [D]etailed historical analysis with all its uncertainties must be employed.[44]

I. Howard Marshall says that interpreters cannot appeal to the doctrine of inspiration to solve historical issues. He reasons that since unbelievers do not share that presupposition, "it is no use to solve historical problems by appeal to a premise which they do not accept."[45] He adds, "the doctrine of inspiration does not prescribe the nature of the reliability which belongs to inspired documents."[46]

Marshall argues that the presence of parables shows that nothing in the doctrine of inspiration requires a belief in the historical reality of any given passage. He writes, "The lesson taught in a parable does not depend upon the historicity of the story but upon the compulsion produced by the storyteller's art."[47] He further writes:

43   Craig Blomberg, *The Historical Reliability of the Gospels* (Downers Grove: InterVarsity Press, 1987), 256 (emphasis added).

44   Ibid., 255 (emphasis added). The question of literary genres will be addressed in the next chapter.

45   I. Howard Marshall, *I Believe in the Historical Jesus* (Grand Rapids: Eerdmans, 1977), 19.

46   Ibid.

47   Ibid.

What the doctrine of inspiration teaches is that the writer was inspired to do what God wanted him to do, and the purpose of his writing is to be learned from a study of the writing itself and not by applying some blanket considerations. So far as the telling of parables is concerned, the recounting of incidents that actually happened is not a necessary part of the process. The point which we have illustrated in this way is of more general application: every part of the Bible must be understood according to its form and purpose, and it cannot be assumed that in every case the writer was attempting to convey historical information, correct in every particular.[48]

For these and other writers like them, the doctrine of inspiration must take a back seat while investigation is conducted according to the standards of historical inquiry. To assume inerrancy as one studies the Bible is to allow preconceptions to color the interpretation and reason in a manner that is inconsistent with true scholarship. The assumption that the Gospel writers intended to convey historical information is not warranted, according to these modern scholars. That methodological approach raises questions that need to be addressed in the next section.

Objections Answered

Should the interpreter set aside his belief in inspiration during his interpretation? Are the Gospels like parables, so that the interpreter is uncertain whether they set forth fact or fiction? These crucial questions require clear answers.

Setting Aside the Presupposition of Inspiration

Several writers have addressed the assertion that inspiration must be set aside in the interest of academic objectivity. For example, Gerhard Maier observes:

48   Ibid., 19-20.

The concept that the Bible must be treated like any other book has plunged theology into an endless chain of perplexities and inner contradictions. This reasoning, which perhaps has a superficial appeal to some, is fundamentally flawed because it adopts a presupposition (namely, that the Bible is like any other book) that is opposed to the true character of the Bible (it is supernaturally inspired by God). Such an interpretive presupposition is sure to produce disaster, because interpretation proceeds from the wrong starting point.[49]

Leon Morris adds:

Too many biblical scholars approach the Bible as though they were atheists or agnostics, or at best deists, holding to the existence of a god who is absent from the world or at least from the writing of the Bible. Whatever they may say in theory about the inspiration of Holy Writ, in practice they treat it as another human document. Not infrequently they pride themselves on doing just this. They suggest that it is necessary to treat the biblical records in the same way as we treat other ancient documents if we are to see them as they are. But this is to overlook the fact that if the Bible is the record of God's revelation it is not just another ancient book.[50]

Those arguments point out the fundamental flaw in the reasoning espoused by Wallace, Blomberg, and Marshall. As a practical matter, they have set aside the inspiration of Scripture—something inherent in the Bible's nature that stands above scholarly judgment. If the Bible truly is God's inerrant Word, then it is the judge of all methods and conclusions. Its truth is not subjected to a higher authority imposed by

49   Gerhard Maier, *The End of the Historical-Critical Method* (St. Louis: Concordia, 1977), 20.

50   Morris, *I Believe in Revelation*, 96.

an autonomous man. Just as a coroner cannot perform an autopsy on a living man, neither can a scholar treat the Bible simply as another human book of antiquity. Its very nature must be accounted for from the outset.

Payne affirms the biblical attitude toward biblical interpretation:

> As a starting point [the believer] holds that the claims of the book itself to be words of God are to be accepted as a working hypothesis and ultimately, that all Scripture is inerrant.... For, rather than eliminating or even claiming to have answered the few seeming discrepancies that do occur, the evangelical simply transfers these to the supernaturalistic column. He places them where man is not to judge for himself, and where God [who is the only One in a position to know] denies him the privilege of saying, "It's not true," because God tells him that Scripture is inerrant. For every critic—the liberal just as much as the evangelical—establishing limits is a matter of faith, either in one's own, internal competence or in another's (Christ's) external authority.[51]

The doctrine of inspiration, then, must be considered in the interpretive process. It does not dictate the proper interpretation of a problem passage, but it does perform a negative function by ruling out factual or historical error in the affirmations of Scripture, whether those affirmations deal with doctrine, morality, history, or science.[52]

Analogy to Parables

It is not legitimate to compare all the narrative portions of the Gospels with parables and from that comparison conclude that the Gospels may not be intending to convey literal, historical truth. Luke expressly states his intention to convey the

---

51   J. Barton Payne, "Higher Criticism and Biblical Inerrancy," in *Inerrancy*, ed. Norman L. Geisler (Grand Rapids: Zondervan, 1980), 92-93.

52   Cf. Feinberg, "The Meaning of Inerrancy," 294.

"exact truth" (τὴν ἀσφάλειαν) for Theophilus (Luke 1:4), and the other Gospel writers do not indicate that they were writing fiction.

The analogy to parables also fails because parables are often clearly identified (e.g., Matt. 13:3) and the purpose for them is explained in the context of the Gospels (e.g., Matt. 13:10-17). Those express contextual factors alert the interpreter to the fact that he is dealing with a parable rather than a historical narrative. The presence of parable markers argues against treating a passage like a parable when those markers are not present in the context. Consequently, it is not valid to argue from parables to general statements about the historical reliability of the rest of the Scriptures, because context does not indicate that the narrative should be taken as anything other than historical fact.

Summary and Conclusions

This chapter has stated the doctrine of inspiration and attempted to work out some of the implications of that doctrine for the interpreter. Because the Scriptures are inspired by God, one must take a deductive approach and interpret the scriptural phenomena from a perspective that upholds the unity and truthfulness of the Bible. Further, the fact that inspiration is *verbal* means that every word is important, and to change a word is to change the meaning of the author. Consequently, every word of Scripture must be treated as significant since it reflects the mind of the Creator.

It was shown that in prophetic, historical, and grammatical detail, the Scripture demonstrates precision that is consistent with its claim to inspiration. These factors show the precarious position of evangelicals who would set aside the presupposition of inspiration as they conduct their study. They proceed from a factually (not just theologically) incorrect starting point that assumes a natural origin of the Bible. Their interpretations are methodologically flawed in a way that undermines their conclusions.

Men ultimately deny Christ when they attempt to follow Him at a distance and warm their hands at the glowing coals of unbelief. The Bible is not inspired and inerrant because some mortal and fallible scholar says so. The Bible is inspired and inerrant as received from the authority of Jesus Christ Himself, who said, "The Scripture cannot be broken" (John 10:35).[53]

---

53   For a pastoral defense of basing biblical authority on the testimony of Christ Himself, see my audio messages, "Jesus Christ and OT Authority" and "Jesus Christ and NT Authority" available at www.truthcommunitychurch.org, delivered on 2/28/2023 and 3/5/2023 respectively.

3

Literary Genre and Gospel Interpretation

 An increasingly popular method of approaching the interpretation of the Gospels is found in the literature on Gospel genre. In recent years, many New Testament scholars have labored to identify the particular genre of literature to which the Gospels belong. The underlying premise is that, if the genre can be identified, the hermeneutical expectations of the documents can be clarified—including the nature of history and theology to expect from the documents.[54]

---

54   Craig L. Blomberg, *Jesus and the Gospels* (Nashville: Broadman & Holman, 1997), 101.

An Introduction to Genre Analysis

Genre analysis divides the books of the New Testament into different categories based on a comparison with other ancient literature written in the surrounding New Testament era. It is based on the premise that the New Testament writers lived in a broader social culture with established patterns of communication that would have been presupposed by author and reader alike. The theory is that the modern interpreter must identify those patterns, or genres, of communication in order to interpret the New Testament properly.[55]

Genre critics have identified several categories of writing to which they believe different parts of the New Testament should be compared, including Gospels, acts (with a small "a"), letters, and apocalypse. Those four forms correspond to the categories in extra-biblical literature of ancient biographical, historical, epistolary, and apocalyptic literature.[56]

Many New Testament scholars examine the characteristics of the Gospels in light of contemporary Greco-Roman literary conventions. Those characteristics would include, among other things, the formal features of the work (such as structure, style, and motifs), the author's intention, the compositional process, and the contents of the work.[57] Hypothetically, at least, such a comparison with the literary genres from the ancient world would help define the manner in which a "Gospel" may be expected to convey truth.[58] In the

55   Cf. David Aune, *The New Testament in Its Literary Environment* (Philadelphia: Westminster, 1987), 13.

56   Ibid. The classification of Revelation as apocalyptic literature has been challenged on the basis that it should more properly be classified as prophetic literature. Robert L. Thomas, "Literary Genre and Hermeneutics of the Apocalypse," *The Master's Seminary Journal* 2 (Spring 1991): 79-97.

57   L. W. Hurtado, "Gospel (Genre)," in *Dictionary of Jesus and the Gospels*, ed. Joel B. Green and Scot McKnight (Downers Grove: InterVarsity, 1992), 277.

58   D. A. Carson, "Recent Developments in the Doctrine of Scripture," in *Hermeneutics, Authority, and Canon*, ed. D. A. Carson and John D. Wood-

pages that follow, the matter of genre criticism will be examined at length.

Definitions of Genre

Before the effect of genre on the interpretation of the Gospels can be discussed, the term "genre" itself must be defined. Surprisingly, there is no uniformity at this most fundamental level. A survey of some suggested definitions is therefore in order.

In his widely recognized book, David Aune defines literary genre as "a group of texts that exhibit a coherent and recurring configuration of literary features involving form (including structure and style), content, and function."[59] Aune distinguishes between "literary genre" and "literary forms." Literary forms exhibit similar recurring features and are primarily "constituent elements of the genres that frame them."[60] Craig Blomberg adopts Aune's definition in an article designed to categorize the genre of entire NT books by comparison with other extant works from the ancient Mediterranean world.[61]

James L. Bailey and Lyle D. Vander Broek take up those terms in reverse order by defining "literary form" before they define "literary genre." They define literary form with two components: First, it designates "the structure or organization of a literary unit or passage" although "style, content, and function might also have to be noted." The second component of literary form is that it "exhibits a structure that is commonly used, one that is found elsewhere in the literature of the period."[62]

When they define the broader term "genre," Bailey and Vander Broek write:

---

bridge (Grand Rapids: Baker, 1995), 36.

59   Aune, *The New Testament in Its Literary Environment*, 13.

60   Ibid.

61   Craig L. Blomberg, "New Testament Genre Criticism for the 1990s," *Themelios* 15 (Jan/Feb 1990): 40.

62   James L. Bailey and Lyle D. Vander Broek, *Literary Forms in the New Testament* (Louisville: Westminster/John Knox Press, 1992), 12-13.

Genres are usually distinguished from literary forms on the basis of length and complexity. Whereas literary forms can be short and structurally simple, the Gospels, the letters, and the one apocalypse (Revelation) in the New Testament are longer pieces that may themselves contain a number of shorter literary forms. Moreover, genres are often defined in terms of content, function, and technique, as well as structure. Certainly the differences between literary form and genre must be kept in mind.[63]

In a later article, Bailey defines "genre" in a *different* way as he writes, "Genres are the conventional and repeatable patterns of oral and written speech, which facilitate interaction among people in specific social situations. Decisive to this basic definition are three aspects: patternedness, social setting, and rhetorical impact."[64]

L. W. Hurtado defines literary genre as "a "category or type of literature, such as biography or novel," and lists the following factors to consider when evaluating the genre of a writing: "formal features (e.g., structure, style, motifs, devices), author's intention, compositional process, setting of author, setting of intended use, and contents."[65]

It is helpful to put the essential elements of these definitions side by side:

63   Ibid., 13-14.

64   James L. Bailey, "Genre Analysis," in *Hearing the New Testament,* ed. Joel B. Green (Grand Rapids: Eerdmans, 1995), 200.

65   Hurtado, "Gospel (Genre)," 277.

Elements of Genre

AUNE	BAILEY & VANDER BROEK	HURTADO	BAILEY (1995)
1. Form	1. Content	1. Formal features	1. Patternedness
a. Structure	2. Function	a. Structure	2. Social setting
b. Style	3. Technique	b. Style	3. Rhetorical impact
2. Content	4. Structure	c. Motifs	
3. Function		d. Devices	
		2. Author's intention	
		3.Compositional process	
		4. Setting of author	
		5. Setting of intended use	
		6. Contents	

A review of these elements shows that there is no scholarly consensus on the proper elements of defining genre, although there are certain areas of overlap. In the first three definitions, the ideas of structure and content are shared, yet at the same time, each definition has its own unique elements. Bailey's definition from 1995 uses none of the same terminology to describe genre, even when compared to his work with Vander Broek. It is possible that his term "social setting" has overlap with Hurtado's settings of "author" and "intended use," but one can only speculate on that conclusion. The impact of these differences on the usefulness of genre criticism will be addressed below.

Genre Classifications of the Gospels

Scholars have proposed several different types of genre classification for the Gospels. These include Hellenistic aretology, lectionaries, biography, and Jewish midrash.[66] While a full dis-

---

66   Robert A. Guelich, *Mark 1-8:26*, Word Biblical Commentary (Dallas: Word, 1989), xix-xxii; Donald Guthrie, *New Testament Introduction*, 4th ed. (Downers Grove: InterVarsity Press, 1990), 17-19. For a helpful survey

cussion of each of these categories is beyond the scope of this book, it is useful to give a brief overview of each of these proposals to develop a picture of the landscape of Gospel genre research in the past several years. An evaluation of each proposal will be given in a subsequent section.

Aretologies

An aretology is a story of miraculous deeds done by a god or by a human hero. Under this genre, the gospels supposedly follow stories about the Greek divine man as a pattern for the gospel narratives about Jesus.[67] The episodes in the life of this past hero are usually embellished or exaggerated to magnify his claim to fame.[68]

Lectionaries

This view asserts that the gospels were patterned after Jewish lectionaries for use in public worship. Proponents of this view submit that the gospels were intentionally designed to augment or replace the Jewish cycle of readings from the Torah. Under this view, the Gospels constitute a liturgical rather than a literary genre.[69]

Proponents of this view make two assumptions: (1) Judaism had developed fixed cycles of readings from Torah and the prophets by the first century AD to provide a pattern for the Gospels; and (2) The Gospel writers adopted the lectionary practice and developed the Gospels into weekly lections with themes corresponding to the Old Testament readings they supplanted.[70]

---

and explanation of the various positions in relation to the Gospels, along with brief critiques of the views, see Blomberg, "New Testament Genre Criticism for the 1990s," 40-42.

67   Guthrie, *New Testament Introduction*, 18.

68   Craig L. Blomberg, *The Historical Reliability of the Gospels* (Downers Grove: Inter-Varsity Press, 1987), 236.

69   Aune, *The New Testament in Its Literary Environment*, 25; Guthrie, *New Testament Introduction*, 18.

70   Aune, *The New Testament in Its Literary Environment*, 25-26.

Biographies

A third view of the Gospels is that they are biographical in nature. Aune defines biography as "a discrete prose narrative devoted exclusively to the portrayal of the whole life of a particular individual perceived as historical."[71] Generally speaking, two types of individuals were featured in those biographies: public men who lived within the structures of society and philosophers who lived outside those structures.[72]

By way of form, most ancient biographies were written in a high and pretentious literary style. The chronological framework of the subject's life generally provided the formal structure for the biography. There were, however, varying degrees of application of both the style and adherence to the general chronology.[73]

This view is supported by the recognition that the Gospels focus on the person and ministry of Jesus in a broadly chronological fashion.[74] Proponents of this view acknowledge that the Gospel writers do not satisfy modern biographical standards given the absence of details regarding the early years of Jesus' life.[75]

Midrash

A fourth view of the genre of the Gospels is developed by Robert Gundry in his commentary on Matthew. He argued that Matthew was patterned after Jewish midrash, which was a form of Old Testament interpretation that often expanded and embellished the Old Testament text. Based on that understanding of Matthew's genre, Gundry concludes that the Gospel regularly describes episodes that did not actually occur but were legendary embellishments of his primary

---

71 Ibid., 29.

72 Ibid., 32-33.

73 Ibid., 34-35.

74 Guelich, *Mark 1–8:26*, xx-xxi.

75 E.g., Blomberg, "New Testament Genre Criticism," 40.

sources, Mark and Q. Under this view, Matthew's theological purpose overrode his concern to convey historical truth with his writing.[76]

The Purpose of Genre Analysis

Genre critics engage in genre analysis because they believe the genre of the gospels is a hermeneutical key to interpretation. They assert that the gospels cannot be properly understood or interpreted unless the genre is recognized and its conventions understood.[77] A brief survey will illustrate the essential role that some authors give to genre analysis in the interpretive process. Hurtado writes:

> Acquaintance with the genre of a writing allows one's understanding of a writing to be guided in light of the features and intentions that characterize the genre. If an author sets out to write in accordance with the conventions and features of a particular genre, it may be comparatively easy to identify the genre of the writing.[78]

Craig Blomberg adds:

> Genre criticism combines the potential of profound

76   Robert H. Gundry, *Matthew: A Commentary on His Handbook for a Mixed Church Under Persecution,* 2d ed. (Grand Rapids: Eerdmans, 1994), 623-640. For a discussion of midrash and a bibliography of works attempting to relate it to the Gospels, see Craig A. Evans, "Midrash," in *Dictionary of Jesus and the Gospels,* ed. Joel B. Green and Scot McKnight, and I. Howard Marshall, consulting ed. (Downers Grove: InterVarsity, 1992), 544-548.

77   David E. Aune, "The Problem of the Genre of the Gospels: A Critique of C. H. Talbert's 'What Is a Gospel?,'" in *Gospel Perspectives: Studies of History and Tradition in the Four Gospels,* ed. R. T. France and David Wenham (Sheffield: JSOT Press, 1981), 9.

78   Hurtado, "Gospel (Genre)," 277. He acknowledges that if the author uses the genre for an unusual purpose, or does not methodically follow the conventions of the genre, it is difficult to employ genre analysis to interpret the document.

insight with the peril of distorting reductionism. To know that a particular writing conforms to certain literary conventions enables the interpreter to avoid exegetical gaffes and more closely to discern the original intentions of an author. But labels always risk blinding the reader to that writing's distinctives—where an author consciously or unconsciously deviates from the expected.[79]

Aune writes:

> Literary genres and forms are not simply neutral containers used as convenient ways to package various types of written communication. They are social conventions that provide contextual meaning for the smaller units of language and text they enclose. The original significance that a literary text had for both author and reader is tied to the genre of that text, so that the meaning of the part is dependent upon the meaning of the whole.[80]

Grant Osborne adds:

> The interpreter examines the potential extrinsic genre-types . . . to determine the intrinsic, originally intended genre [that] helps one to delineate the proper hermeneutical principles to employ in seeking the meaning of a passage. Through it one can discover the allusions to other ancient ideas which the writer and his readers presupposed, but we cannot. . . . Genre is more than a means of classifying literary types; it is an epistemological tool for unlocking meaning in individual texts.[81]

79 Blomberg, "New Testament Genre Criticism," 40. Blomberg believes that the genre of the NT writings can be sufficiently identified to aid in interpretation, but they have unique features which set them apart from anything found in extra-biblical writings.

80 Aune, *The New Testament in Its Literary Environment*, 13.

81 Grant R. Osborne, "Genre Criticism—Sensus Literalis," in *Hermeneu-*

These comments show that genre critics believe genre criticism is *indispensable* to interpretation. Indeed, they assert that the identification of genre *precedes* the interpretive process, because proper exegesis can only take place in the context of a properly identified genre. James Bailey, for example, says, "[W]hen reading the NT we will not appreciate what is going on with biblical texts if we do not recognize the operative genres and their specific uses."[82] Genre, it is argued, provides contextual meaning for the smaller units of language and text they enclose and was assumed by the original authors and readers. As a result, the meaning of the part is dependent upon the meaning of the whole.[83]

An Evaluation of Genre Analysis of the Gospels

The above comments from genre critics are far-reaching. To argue that the Gospels *cannot* be understood without genre analysis is to conceal the life and deeds of Jesus Christ from those unfamiliar with genre classifications. The implications of that claim should therefore be scrutinized closely to assess its validity.

Definitions of Genre

The first observation that strikes the interpreter about genre analysis is the lack of definitional uniformity. The sometimes-overlapping, sometimes-conflicting elements of the definition of "genre" indicate a lack of maturity in the field of study. The problem is illustrated when an author like James Bailey changes his own definitions of key terms in a matter of few years. No objective standards guide the writers on this topic. An unbiased observer would be decidedly unimpressed with such subjectivity.

---

tics, Inerrancy, and the Bible, ed. Earl D. Radmacher and Robert D. Preus (Grand Rapids: Zondervan, 1984), 177, 182.

82   Bailey, "Genre Analysis," 198.

83   Aune, *The New Testament in Its Literary Environment,* 13.

At the very least, this lack of uniformity should cause genre critics to qualify their assertions that genre analysis is indispensable to the hermeneutical process. It is difficult to believe that the reader cannot understand the New Testament without the benefit of a discipline that has not yet determined how to define itself. Those who press the role of genre risk compromising the perspicuity of Scripture, which asserts that the biblical writers communicated their meaning clearly so that it would make wise even the simple (cf. Ps. 19:7).[84]

Genre Classifications of the Gospels

Not only do they disagree at the definitional level, genre critics disagree on the specific classification of the Gospels. The following discussion will briefly evaluate the various proposals.

Aretologies

The theory that the Gospels follow the pattern of Hellenistic aretologies has not enjoyed much support in recent years. Craig Blomberg sums up its weaknesses:

> [T]he evidence from several recent studies suggests that no clear stereotype of a 'divine man' predated the second century A.D. Among those called divine men during the time of or before the writing of the gospels, no consistent pattern of miracle-working activity emerges, and close parallels with specific events in Jesus' life are rare. When the patterns become more consistent and the parallels closer, several generations have already elapsed since the life of Christ, so that the evangelists cannot be accused of moulding their stories to fit a stereotyped form of Greek 'divinization.'[85]

---

84   Cf. Robert L. Thomas, "Impact of Historical Criticism on Hermeneutics," in *The Jesus Crisis*, ed. Robert L. Thomas and F. David Farnell (Grand Rapids: Kregel, 1998), 328-330.

85   Blomberg, *Historical Reliability*, 86; cf. Guthrie, *New Testament Introduction*, 18.

Based on Blomberg's discussion, it would appear that chronological factors would eliminate aretologies from serious consideration as the source of the genre of the Gospels. Obviously, the genre would need to predate the writing of the Gospels to provide a pattern for them.

Lectionaries

The proposal that the Gospels were structured to replace Jewish Sabbath or festival readings from the Torah suffers from several objections. First, the assumption that Jewish lectionary practices were in place by the first century A.D. goes beyond that which the evidence warrants. Even Jewish scholars are not willing to make confident assertions about the status of the lectionaries at that time, which illustrates the difficulty for Christians to argue that the Gospels were patterned after Jewish lectionaries.[86]

The sacrosanct position necessary to use a book as a standard for worship services also makes it unlikely that the Gospels were intended to replace the Torah *immediately*. Even if that replacement occurred at a later date, it would not explain the genre of the Gospels. Finally, the lectionary proposal does not explain the use of Jesus' life as the lectionary framework nor for the thematic unity of the Gospels.[87] Upon examination, then, many of the supposed parallels between the Jewish readings and the text of the gospels are not close enough to be convincing.[88]

Biographies

The Gospels do bear some resemblance to the popular biographies of the Greco-Roman era. Luke's preface in 1:1-4 has similarity to the prefaces of Greco-Roman literary works. The Gospels also promote a particular "hero," as was the tendency in Roman biographies as well.[89] Hurtado suggests that the

86 Guthrie, *New Testament Introduction*, 19.

87 Aune, *The New Testament in Its Literary Environment*, 27.

88 Guthrie, *New Testament Introduction*, 19.

89 Hurtado, "Gospel (Genre)," 278.

Gospels follow Greco-Roman motifs of "heroic martyrdom," important teaching and events set at meal scenes, and the motif of the teacher and his disciples.[90]

Yet the parallel with Greco-Roman biography is by no means precise. More central to the Gospels than the similarities mentioned above are the Gospel writers' repeated references to the Old Testament and the exalted place of Jesus as Messiah. These distinctive themes show that the Gospels are not merely patterned after contemporary literature. The authors demonstrated independence in their thinking and stylistic devices that limits the significance of a point-for-point comparison with Greco-Roman biographies. The unique subject of Jesus Christ and the setting of the early church provided the immediate setting of the writing of the Gospels, not the literary activities of the broader Greco-Roman era.[91]

Another frequently mentioned observation about the Gospels is that they do not fit the pattern of modern biographies. For example, Mark and John provide no details regarding Jesus' birth, childhood, or young adult life. The main focus is on the comparatively brief portion of His public ministry and the events surrounding His death and resurrection. Even at that, the material is often arranged topically instead of chronologically.[92]

These significant distinctions should restrict any effort to classify the genre of the Gospels with ancient biography. Even more, it should caution the interpreter about imposing hermeneutical principles derived from secular biographies upon the Gospels in light of those differences.

Midrash

Many conservatives reacted strongly against Robert Gundry's proposal that Matthew patterned his Gospel after Jewish midrash. Gundry's position requires Matthew, an apostle and eyewitness to the events of Christ, to feel free to embellish what

90   Ibid.
91   Ibid.
92   Blomberg, *Jesus and the Gospels*, 107.

Mark and Q contained so he could convey his own emphases. His proposal that Matthew described events that never occurred was judged to be incompatible with inerrancy, and ultimately led to his resignation from the Evangelical Theological Society.[93] Even apart from those considerations, it further assumes that Matthew's readers were sufficiently familiar with the events of the life of Christ to be able to distinguish historical fact from Matthew's fiction.[94] Guthrie adds the following critique:

> The major problem here is to determine what any particular writer means by midrash, since the word is used in a variety of different ways. Gundry sometimes uses it of the whole gospel, sometimes of parts of it. He seems to treat the midrashic elements as unhistorical embellishments. But the question arises whether in fact there was such a literary practice in Jewish approaches to history. It is highly unlikely that the supposition that Matthew had such a clear-cut pattern can be substantiated.[95]

The Uniqueness of the Gospels

In addition to the foregoing qualitative differences, the Gospels also have their own unique literary characteristics. These features distinguish the Gospels from other contemporary writings, and must be considered in any attempt to classify their genre.

Anonymity

Each of the Gospels in their present form is written anonymously. Although modern readers are accustomed to attributing the various Gospels to Matthew, Mark, Luke, or John, those

---

93   Robert L. Thomas, "Historical Criticism and the Evangelical: Another View," *Journal of the Evangelical Theological Society* 43 (March 2000): 99.

94   Blomberg, "New Testament Genre Criticism for the 1990s," 41.

95   Guthrie, *New Testament Introduction*, 19.

designations of authorship derive from superscriptions that were attached after the Gospels had been written, probably early in the second century AD.[96]

That anonymity should be contrasted with the normal pattern of Greco-Roman biographies that were normally written in the names of real or fictitious/pseudonymous authors. Any assessment of Gospel genre must address this issue.[97] The Gospel writers were not calling attention to themselves and did not see themselves primarily as authors for a general audience. Rather, they considered themselves as "servants of the word" (Luke 1:2) who made the message prominent as they hid themselves in the background.[98]

The "Literaturization" of the Gospels

The uniqueness of the Gospels is also illustrated in the changes that were made to them during the copying process after the Gospel writers had completed the autographs. These changes include the addition of the superscriptions to the Gospels, which brought them into greater conformity with the Greco-Roman standards of avoiding anonymous works. Also, some copyists of the Gospels inserted stylistic features such as spacing, use of the iota adscript, and paragraph marks, which paleographers attribute to literary hands.[99] The desire to conform the Gospels to prevailing literary practices indicates the originals did *not* conform to existing practices. That is a lethal blow to the entire foundation of genre analysis.

Further evidence of the literary uniqueness of the Gospels

---

96 Ned B. Stonehouse, *Origins of the Synoptic Gospels* (Grand Rapids: Eerdmans, 1963), 15-18.

97 Aune, "The Problem of the Genre of the Gospels," 44. Not all genre critics have heeded Aune's admonition in this regard. See, e.g., Bailey, "Genre Analysis," 199-212.

98 Cf. Hurtado, "Gospel (Genre)," 279.

99 Aune, "The Genre of the Gospels," 45. Aune also suggests that Matthew and Luke are evidence of this movement because of their effort to increase the literary sophistication of Mark and their addition of narratives and genealogies to Mark's work. That suggestion will carry weight only with those who hold to Markan priority and literary dependence, a position not adopted here.

is found in the writings of Papias and Justin Martyr. Papias defended the literary character of Mark against unknown critics, and demonstrated familiarity with rhetorical terms and conventions in his defense. Likewise, Justin sought to classify the Gospels as "memoirs" of the apostles in a separate effort to link the Gospels with a known literary type. From those writings in the early church, it is apparent that there was a concerted effort to defend Mark's Gospel against attacks on its perceived sub-literary character. That defense would have been unnecessary, and indeed superfluous, if the Gospels had conformed with prevailing literary practices.[100]

The Language and Style of the Gospels

The Gospels must also be distinguished from their contemporary counterparts on the basis of their language and style. Aune writes, "With few exceptions, the literary heritage of the Greco-Roman world reflects the culture, values and tastes of the upper classes. In that highly structured elitist society, there was a correlation between social level and literary culture."[101] By contrast, the Gospels better reflect the language and style of the common man, either as found in the papyri or the language reflecting their minority group status.[102]

This difference in language and style has not been given sufficient weight in discussion of genre analysis. As discussed above, one of the axioms of genre criticism is that the genre of the Gospels reflects one of the prevailing patterns of literature of the times.[103] However, it is difficult to equate the genre of the Gospels with the genre of then-contemporary literature when their language and style differ significantly. Such differences would affect not only the literary quality of the work, but also the social expectations of the readers as they read the Gospels and recognized the differences with prevailing literature. Many modern genre critics do not adequately address Aune's

100 Ibid.
101 Ibid., 47.
102 Ibid.
103 See above, 31-34.

warnings on the comparison of the language and style of the Gospels with contemporary literature.[104] The Gospel writers would not have imitated the genre of literature for the elite while using common language to express their thoughts.

Formal Parallels, Material Differences
As one considers the uniqueness of the Gospels, he must proceed cautiously even when he observes parallels in structure or style with other ancient literature. There is an ever-present "danger of parallelomania" which draws conclusions from surface similarities that disappear upon further investigation.[105] The existence of parallels is no guarantee that the writers of the Gospels *intended* their works to be understood in accordance with those secular conventions. That is particularly evident when one considers that key events in Jesus' life—such as the resurrection and ascension—have no true parallel in Greco-Roman literature despite surface similarities that may exist.[106]

Genre and Historical Standards

The discussion of Gospel genre bears on the discussion of *ipsissima vox* because genre critics claim that genre classification influences the historical expectations the interpreter should bring to the text. If the interpreter determines that the Gospel writer employed a genre that did not intend historical accuracy, then one should not read the events described in the Gospel narratives as actual time-and-space historical occurrences.[107]

104   See, e.g., Hurtado, "Gospel (Genre)," 279-281; Bailey and Vander Broek, *Literary Forms*, 91-98.

105   The term "parallelomania" refers to "that extravagance among scholars which first overdoes the supposed similarity in passages and then proceeds to describe source and derivation as if implying literary connection flowing in an inevitable or predetermined direction" (Samuel Sandmel, "Parallelomania," *Journal of Biblical Literature* 81 [March 1962]: 1).

106   Aune, "The Genre of the Gospels," 47-48.

107   E.g., Gundry, *Matthew*, 627-640.

J. Barton Payne writes:

> Some interpreters consider themselves advocates of
> inerrancy, but are willing, nevertheless, to grant the
> existence of erroneous statements in Scripture about the
> circumstances of the origin of a given passage. The errors
> are due to the literary genre, or form (namely, the Gospels)
> in which the statements occur. Since the Bible contains
> such literary figures as hyperbole and parable, both of
> which are fictional, could it not be, they argue, that the
> Gospels form a particular type of Christian literary genre,
> in which a redactor, in the interests of his theological
> message, reshapes the historical tradition he has received?
> The message is thus said to prevail over historical accuracy,
> with no attempt to deceive being intended by the author/
> redactor. In other words, the question is simply one of
> exegesis and hermeneutics, not of errancy.
>
> While such a reconstruction is theoretically possible,
> it would seem to be highly inappropriate for at least the
> narrative portions of the Gospels. An author who intends
> to use a fictional form should make this fact, as well as
> his reason for using such a form, clear to his readers.
> The four Gospels, however, contain no clues that they
> are fictional in the sense claimed by those using the
> methods of current redaction criticism. They assert just
> the opposite (Luke 1:1-4), and for 1900 years readers have
> been impressed by their form as one that intends and
> assumes historicity."[108]

Payne's thoughts deserve a broader hearing than they have
been granted to date. By all accounts, the advent of genre analysis is quite new. The newness should warn the interpreter

---

108   J. Barton Payne, "Higher Criticism and Biblical Inerrancy," in *Inerrancy*, ed. Norman L. Geisler (Grand Rapids: Zondervan, 1980), 98. By
contrast, the Gospel writers *do* disclose that they are presenting a *selective* account of the life of Christ (John 20:30-31). The Gospel writers did
not record everything they had seen and heard; however, their selective
reporting was consistent with what was actually said and done.

against overturning 1,900 years of conservative scholarship that understood the Gospels as straightforward historical accounts of the life of Jesus.

Summary and Conclusions

As the foregoing survey has shown, scholars have differed widely over the interpretation of the genre of the Gospels. They differ not only on the definitional level but also on the identification of the supposed genre of the Gospels. Multiple definitions of genre, and multiple identifications of types of Gospel genre, illustrate the comparative infancy of the discipline. Perhaps further study will bring greater clarity to a field presently beset by wide disagreement. For now, the reverent student of Scripture will substantially discount the academic boasts of men who claim they have discovered a key to unlock meaning that had been concealed and unnoticed for nearly two thousand years.

Stated differently, genre critics overreach when they insist that genre analysis is indispensable to understanding the text. Indeed, one writer concedes that, for the Synoptic Gospels at any rate, "There are no indications that the author was consciously shaping his work in the light of any literary precedents or patterns."[109]

That admission begs a crucial question: If the goal of interpretation is to determine authorial intent, and the author did not consciously employ a genre style, how can genre be indispensable at arriving at the meaning of the text? Those who acknowledge this difficulty say that genre analysis can inform "the general climate" that contributed to the writing of the Gospel.[110] Such weak assertions belie the consistent overstate-

---

109 Hurtado, "Gospel (Genre)," 279. How firmly Hurtado holds that position is open for question, because he later writes, "It is likely that the Evangelists consciously and perhaps more often, unconsciously reflected features of Greco-Roman popular literature" ("Gospel (Genre)," 282). Such shifting conclusions highlight the subjectivity of genre analysis.

110 Ibid., 280.

ment that genre analysis is a precondition to understanding the Gospels.[111]

Consequently, the interpreter should approach genre analysis with suspicion that gives greater priority to the perspecuity of Scripture for the common reader. The Gospel writers chose their literary forms under the inspiration of the Holy Spirit, and thus wrote uniquely. The words of Guthrie are salutary:

> Whereas it is right to examine any other possible parallels, there must always be a question mark over parallels in view of the special character of the gospels. The uniqueness of the central person in the gospels places the records in a class of their own. The acknowledgment of this fact does not place them beyond critical examination, but it should urge caution before too readily assuming that they can without any conditions be placed alongside secular literature.[112]

The key question is not how extra-biblical literature influenced the Gospels, but how the Gospels influenced extra-biblical literature.[113] The Gospels have a transcendent nature due to their divine origin and their divine subject, Jesus Christ. The Gospel writers were not subject to the restraints of the culture of their day because they wrote under the direct inspiration of the Holy Spirit. That supernatural element means that the scriptural authors would not *necessarily* have followed the literary conventions of their time. They were unlike any authors of their time as they wrote about God the Son under the inspiration of God the Spirit. Indeed,

---

111   While one could conceivably suggest that genre had a *subconscious* influence on the writing of the Gospels, the interpreter cannot ascertain that influence apart from clear indications in the text. Thus, there would seem to be little profit in speculating on the subconscious influence of genre when there are no genre markers in the text itself.

112   Guthrie, *New Testament Introduction*, 21.

113   Ibid., 16.

they were unlike any authors *in all of human history*.

Thus, it is not legitimate to lump the Gospels into a pre-existing category of ancient literature. The human writers were unique and the end product—an inspired writing—was likewise unique. An analysis of genre that fails to reckon with these qualitative differences between the Gospels and extra-biblical literature has failed to deal with the most material of all facts.

Inspiration matters.

4

"Ipsissima Vox"
and Ancient
Historiography

Ipsissima vox proponents usually support their position by asserting that it is consistent with the general standards of recording speeches in ancient secular history. Supporters argue that classic historians did not use modern quotation marks to set off precise quotations. As a result, the accepted practice was to be "faithful to the meaning of the original utterance," while the exact phrasing was left to the discretion of the writer. Writers who so framed their quotations would not be accused of inaccurate reporting.[114]

---

114   Craig L. Blomberg, *The Historical Reliability of the Gospels* (Downers Grove: InterVarsity Press, 1987), 118.

The Recording of Speeches in Ancient History

To support that assertion, *ipsissima vox* advocates routinely refer to a famous statement by the ancient historian Thucydides (c. 460-400 B.C.), who was a pioneer in the writing of history. One authority states, "Readers of all opinions will probably agree that [Thucydides] saw more truly, inquired more responsibly, and reported more faithfully than any other ancient historian."[115] Thucydides explained his historical method in the introduction to his work, describing the nature of his speeches as follows:

> In this history I have made use of set speeches some of which were delivered just before and others during the war. I have found it difficult to remember the precise words used in the speeches which I listened to myself and my various informants have experienced the same difficulty; so my method has been, while keeping as closely as possible to the general sense of the words that were actually used, to make the speakers say what, in my opinion, was called for by each situation.[116]

Ipsissima vox advocates rely heavily on Thucydides' acknowledgment that he did not use the "precise words" in the speeches found in his history, but rather kept as closely as possible to the "general sense" of what was said. They suggest that Thucydides' practice established the standard for recording speeches in subsequent historical writing up to the time of the Gospels. Since the Gospel writers were products of their milieu, they should be expected to write in accordance with the historical standards of their time, which only called for adherence to the general sense of the speeches, not their

115   Henry Theodore Wade-Gery, John Dewar Denniston, and Simon Hornblower, "Thucydides," *Oxford Classical Dictionary*, 3d ed. (Oxford: Oxford University Press, 1996), 1519.

116   Thucydides, *History of the Peloponnesian War*, 1.22, rev. ed., translated by Rex Warner (New York: Penguin Books, 1972), 47.

actual words.[117] Consequently, the modern reader of the Gospels should *expect* to find primarily paraphrases and a summary of Jesus' words, not His actual words themselves.[118]

Ipsissima vox proponents differ in some degree over the level of verbal precision that the reader can find in the Gospels based on the historiographic standards in place at the time. Darrell Bock, for example, believes that Thucydides' words established the pattern for the Gospel writers, which was to have "a concern for accuracy in reporting the gist of what had been said, even if the exact words were not remembered or recorded."[119]

Daniel Wallace, on the other hand, argues for a broader view of *ipsissima vox* in the Gospels. He agrees generally with Bock's assertion about Thucydides, and believes the famous historian did not make up his speeches *ex nihilo*, but did take substantial liberty with the wording, style, and diction of the speeches. He was committed to a faithful representation of the basic meaning of the speeches, though the language was his own.[120]

Wallace differs from Bock, however, because he suggests that the Gospel writers may have followed a *less* rigorous standard than even Thucydides. According to Wallace, the standard of historical reporting declined in secular history in the centuries between Thucydides and the Gospel writers. Consequently, the immediate historical context of the Gospel writers reflected even less concern for verbal precision in recording

---

117   One writer suggests that scholars who rely on Thucydides to establish "the" historiographic standard for recording speeches do so at their own peril because of the many interpretive difficulties in the text. Stanley E. Porter, "Thucydides 1.22.1 and Speeches in Acts: Is There a Thucydidean View?" *Novum Testamentum* 32 (April 1990): 121-142.

118   Darrell L. Bock, "The Words of Jesus in the Gospels: Live, Jive, or Memorex?," in *Jesus Under Fire*, ed. Michael J. Wilkins and J. P. Moreland (Grand Rapids: Zondervan, 1995), 78-79; Daniel B. Wallace, "An *Apologia* for a Broad View of *Ipsissima Vox*," paper presented at the 51st Annual Meeting of the Evangelical Theological Society (Danvers, MA: November, 1999): 1-5.

119   Bock, "The Words of Jesus," 78-79.

120   Wallace, "An *Apologia*," 3.

speeches than Thucydides' quotation would suggest.[121]

Wallace also refines the position by suggesting that one can expect differences between the Gospel writers. For example, one would expect less precision from John than Luke, because John allegedly had less concern for historical accuracy.[122] Wallace advocates greater leeway for the Gospel writers to adjust the words of Christ than Bock's published views. While there is substantial overlap in the two positions, there are sufficient distinctions to justify a separate analysis of the views that Bock and Wallace offer.

Evangelicals, Ancient History, and "Ipsissima Vox"

The View of Darrell Bock

In his article, Bock was writing primarily in response to the Jesus Seminar, which believed that the Gospel writers created sayings and put them on Jesus' lips.[123] The Jesus Seminar was an attempt to shred the credibility of Scripture in reporting the words of Jesus, using the tools of historical criticism to do so. Bock was writing to uphold a greater standard of accuracy for the words of Jesus than the Seminar allowed.

Verbal Precision of Speeches in Secular History
In his discussion of ancient historiographic standards, Bock relies *exclusively* on Charles Fornara's work *The Nature of History in Ancient Greece and Rome*[124] to establish his position.[125]

---

121   Ibid., 4.

122   Ibid., 4-5.

123   Bock, "The Words of Jesus," 75.

124   Charles William Fornara, *The Nature of History in Ancient Greece and Rome* (Berkeley: University of California Press, 1983). Bock may also be influenced by A. W. Mosley, "Historical Reporting in the Ancient World," *New Testament Studies* 12 (1965-1966): 10-26, although he does not cite Mosley in his article in *Jesus Under Fire*.

125   Bock, "The Words of Jesus," 78-79. Bock has only four footnotes

Fornara argues that a genuine "core" of speeches is recorded in Greek history from the end of the sixth to the first century B.C. He also "cautiously" asserts that those speeches in Roman history are substantially trustworthy from the time of the Second Punic War (c. 218-201 B.C.) to the end of the fourth century A.D.[126]

Fornara traces the attitudes of ancient historians from the time of Thucydides through the following centuries to support his assertions. Following a description of historians from Thucydides into imperial times, Fornara concludes that while the importance of speeches in history diminished in the centuries following Thucydides, "the more important principle of reporting the main points of what had actually been said remained (theoretically) an unquestioned rule through Hellenistic times at least."[127]

Fornara notes a change with the establishment of the Roman Empire. Some historians were rhetorical in nature, and while there may be some germ of the actual speeches in their record, it was not a matter of importance to them to preserve what was actually said. Other historians demonstrated fidelity to the substance of the speech while still using stylistic freedom. That freedom included the liberty to rearrange, condense, and to give arguments in what seemed to him the most appropriate form and order.[128]

In reviewing the application of that theory in historical practice, Fornara states why he believes that the ancients proved faithful to that doctrine.[129] He examines the practice of Thucydides, Polybius, and Tacitus in support of his position. Based on this broad examination of evidence, Fornara argues for a general reliability of ancient speeches, even if

---

in this section titled "The Greco-Roman Historical Tradition," all of which refer to Fornara's work.

126   Fornara, *The Nature of History,* 168.

127   Ibid., 151.

128   Ibid., 152-153.

129   Ibid., 143.

the historians were not *invariably* reliable.[130] He acknowledges that most historians would find the speeches less reliable than what Fornera himself asserts.[131]

Secular History and Gospel Speeches
When he writes on the words of Jesus in the Gospels, Bock adopts Fornara's arguments and applies them to the Gospel writers, even though Fornara himself does not consider the Gospels in his work. Bock believes that Fornara is describing the pattern of careful ancient historians, and finds a parallel in Luke 1:1-4. He writes, " The Evangelists were able to search out what Jesus did and said because they had access to people and communities who had been exposed to Jesus or his intimate followers."[132]

In one sense, it is easy to see why Bock would adopt Fornara's historiographic standards and apply them to the Scriptures. Fornara makes a credible case for the substantial trustworthiness of the accounts of speeches in antiquity. If that standard is established, and one assumes that the Gospel writers operated in conjunction with the historiographic norms of the day, then Bock has arguably presented a *prima facie* case that the Bible is substantially more reliable than the Jesus Seminar concluded.

The View of Daniel Wallace

Wallace also argues that ancient history provides the level of precision to expect from the Gospels. However, he leans toward the understanding that Thucydides was unique in his devotion to accuracy, even though he summarized and modified the speeches he recorded.[133] Later historians may have been less precise. Wallace reasons:

130   Ibid., 160.
131   Ibid., 142.
132   Bock, "The Words of Jesus," 79.
133   Wallace, *"An Apologia,"* 2 (emphasis in original).

Now if the genre of the gospels is in keeping historiographically with the best of ancient historians, should we not *expect* the gospel writers to employ at times a broad use of *ipsissima vox*? . . . And even if Luke consciously followed a Thucydidian model, the other evangelists, especially John, hardly seem to.[134]

Wallace specifies the direction he wants to take the *ipsissima vox* position. His view allows for changes and additions to the words of Jesus, even though the Gospel writers are presenting them as words from Jesus' lips. Wallace writes:

1. If Luke felt certain liberties in the speeches he recorded, John may well have done so much more.[135]

2. Matthew made changes in the words of Jesus.[136]

3. Luke "has actually slightly altered the meaning of Jesus' words here."[137]

4. However we regard Luke's addition, that it is an *addition* is generally conceded.[138]

134   Ibid., 4-5.

135   Ibid., 5 (referring to the historiographical standards of the Gospel writers).

136   Ibid., 8 (referring to the rich young ruler in Matthew 19:16-17). Wallace suggests that Matthew changed Mark's account "to deflect some christological problems that Mark's representation could involve."

137   Ibid., 10 (referring to the words, "I have not come to call the righteous, but sinners *to repentance*" in Luke 5:32; the italicized words being Luke's additions).

138   Ibid., 11 (also referring to Luke 5:32). Wallace is aware of the significance of these remarks, and attempts to qualify them by saying, "I am *not* saying that Luke is wrong to add this phrase, nor that repentance was not implicit in Jesus' utterance; I am simply suggesting that the emphasis shifts a bit in Luke." That qualification is disingenuous at best. Wallace still asserts that Luke recorded *as Jesus' words* things that Jesus never said.

5. It seems difficult to claim that 'And if she divorces her husband and marries another, she commits adultery' really belongs to Jesus' utterance.[139]

6. To sum up, there seems to be evidence in the synoptic gospels that, on occasion, words are deliberately added to the original sayings of Jesus."[140]

Have Bock and Wallace proven their case in favor of the *ipsissima vox* position? Suffice to say, Thucydides would blush at their chutzpah.

A Critique of Evangelical Views of Ancient History and "Ipsissima Vox"

Historical Assessment

The Gospels and Ancient Historiography
Darrell Bock's reliance on Fornara's statements regarding ancient historiography undermines an orthodox view of inspiration. First, it is not at all clear that Fornara himself is accurate in his assessment of the reliability of ancient records of speeches. Numerous historians believe the standard is substantially *lower* than Fornara argues. The Thucydidean principle may have established an ideal, but whether it was followed in *practice* is another matter altogether.

Some historians have argued that Thucydides himself did not follow the practice of recording the main substance of the speeches found in his writings. In some places, Thucydides demonstrably did not follow the actual content of the speeches that he records. The *Oxford Classical Dictionary* has these comments:

139   Ibid., 12.
140   Ibid.

It is much debated whether [Thucydides made his statement about his speeches] early or late [in his career]; and it has been much explained away. But it is unreasonable to doubt that from the start Thucydides took notes himself, or sought for hearers' notes, of the speeches he considered important. But since he used speeches dramatically, to reveal the workings of men's minds and the impact of circumstance, it is clear that verbatim reports would not have served even if he could have managed to get them, and he was bound to compromise (unconsciously) between dramatic and literal truth. It is likely that, as his technique developed, dramatic truth would tend to prevail; it is tempting to put his profession of method early, a young man's intention.[141]

Other writers dispute the notion that subsequent historians followed the Thucydidean principle in their writings. They maintain that later writers strayed far from Thucydides' standard of accuracy and wrote scarcely believable accounts of speeches. Ferdinand Schevill maintains that some ancient historians obviously made no effort to convey the true substance of the speeches. He writes:

The historians who came after Thucydides throughout the long succession of classical centuries were so hypnotized by what they considered the charms of rhetoric that *they tended to hide and even black out the facts they had set out to present* behind a blinding curtain of verbal fireworks. It has been universally agreed that the speeches of Thucydides carry so different a content from those of all other classical historians that they rate

141   Wade-Gery, Denniston, and Hornblower, "Thucydides," 1518. The authors give several examples to support their assertion. They do not reject Thucydides' speeches as fiction, and indeed, believe that Thucydides tried to recreate real occasions. One does not have to reject all of Thucydides' speeches to recognize that he may not have always followed his standard in actual practice.

as a contribution unique of its kind. [142]

M. I. Finley says that Thucydides had a passion for accuracy in history, but he was "an exceedingly lonely figure in the history of ancient historical writing, for not one man after him, among either the Greek historians or the Roman, shared his passion."[143] And Mortimer Chambers, Professor Emeritus of Ancient History at the University of California, Los Angeles, writes:

> After [the time of Thucydides] the integrity of speeches in narrative dropped off considerably. Dionysius of Halicarnassus, for example, who wrote about the time of Jesus or a bit earlier . . . gave way to fantastic, florid speeches about which no one could say, as Thucydides said of his speeches, that they tried to give a summary of what was actually said.[144]

One need not resolve this dispute among historical experts to see that the "standards of ancient historiography" are not as well defined as Bock's article suggests. Bock's research is far too narrow and biased to provide a basis to dismiss the biblical words of Jesus. It seems that Bock follows Fornara's analysis because it supports his conclusions, not because Fornara represents a consensus on ancient historiographic standards. At the very least, one must conclude that Fornara's views are broadly disputed among modern historians. Bock's exclusive reliance on Fornara is a failure of serious scholarship.

That weakness in Bock's position is compounded as one investigates Fornara's position further. Bock conveniently omits some of Fornara's conclusions that are critical to the

---

142   Ferdinand Schevill, *Six Historians* (Chicago: University of Chicago Press, 1956), 19 (emphasis added).

143   M. I. Finley, *Aspects of Antiquity*, (New York: The Viking Press, 1968), 49.

144   From personal correspondence with Dr. Mortimer Chambers, August 10, 2000.

evangelical committed to the inspiration of Scriptures. While Fornara adopts a *generally* high view toward secular speeches in ancient history, he acknowledges that the historical standard of the time often did not even keep to the *gist* of the speech:

> *Always* there was the admixture of the imagination and intellect of the historian, and it obviously increased in the degree that the recollection of speeches actually delivered grew dimmer, or the same speech was recast by a succession of authors to suit the best rhetorical theory. The vagaries of the historical tradition accessible to the writer also facilitated *self-deception*. Knowledge that a speech actually had been delivered, the conviction that a speech must have been delivered, the inference that a speech probably was delivered because it was required, are easy gradations leading to *unintentional perjury, and it would be rash to deny the occasional occurrence of such defalcations as these.* . . . But these imperfections in the practice of the historians should not detract from the basic integrity of their approach.[145]

The reverent student of the Gospels should not miss that Fornara's standard allows for "self-deception," "unintentional perjury," and "defalcations" in the historical writings. While that may be acceptable in the realm of secular history, it cannot be reconciled with an orthodox commitment to the inspiration and inerrancy of Scripture—the Scriptures that assert their perfection (Ps. 19:7), truth (John 17:17), and inviolability (Matt. 5:18).

To be sure, Bock does not explicitly argue for such imperfections in Scripture. But he still has set up a Trojan horse outside the gates of biblical reliability. If Fornara is correct about the historiographic standards, and Bock is correct that the New Testament authors wrote in accordance with those standards, then the student of Scripture should not only expect

145 Fornara, *The Nature of History*, 167-68 (emphasis added).

paraphrases and summaries of Jesus' words in the Gospels, he should also expect the kind of errors that Fornara adopts. Bock's analysis is defenseless against that conclusion.

The consequences of Wallace's article are even more significant. Wallace is willing to accept a view of ancient historiography that allows for even greater liberties than suggested by Fornara.[146] One can only ask where Wallace's view will lead, if Bock's adoption of Fornara's *higher* view allows for self-deception, defalcations, and unintentional perjury. One need not be "deeply entrenched in bibliological presuppositions"[147] to question his comments. They undermine the historicity of the Gospels and are inconsistent with inerrancy. Once the interpreter allows the Gospel writers to pass off their own additions and changes as words from the lips of Jesus, there is nothing standing between him and a denial of the historicity of Jesus' words. Let the student beware.

How Does "History" Work?

Before the next chapter assesses Darrell Bock's treatment of certain parallel passages in the Synoptic Gospels, it is also necessary to comment on his presuppositions about the nature of history, because those presuppositions color his arguments in support of *ipsissima vox*. He sees historical events as having an unfolding meaning in light of subsequent events, as he writes:

> History is not a static entity. Neither are the sayings that belong to it and describe its events. Historical events and sayings do not just happen and then sit fossilized with a static meaning. As events in history proceed, they develop their meaning through the interconnected events that give history its sense of flow. Later events impact how previous

146 Cf. Wallace, "An *Apologia*," 4.

147 Wallace uses that phrase to explain why he refuses to interact with those holding to synoptic literary independence. He essentially calls those who hold to literary independence "right-wing fundamentalists" and compares them to radical liberals because "both are driven by their presuppositions" ("An *Apologia*," 19-20, n. 76). Such ad hominem arguments are sadly common in New Testament scholarship.

events and sayings are understood, seen, and appreciated. Even when those earlier events had conscious intentions tied to them when they occurred, what takes place later influences how those earlier events and the things said about them are seen and understood.[148]

This discussion is admittedly elusive. But it is important for understanding Bock's theory of *ipsissima vox*. He holds that since the meaning of words and events can change over time, there is less need to preserve the actual words that were uttered on an occasion, since different words may more accurately explain the meaning in light of subsequent events.

Bock's approach thus blurs the distinction between the time-and-space historical event and the interpretation placed on that event at a later time. In so doing, he violates historical principles set down by historians such as Earle E. Cairns, who carefully distinguish between the use of "history" to describe a historical *incident* and the use of "history" to describe the historical *interpretation* that a historian applies to the incident at a later time. The historical *incident* is an actual event in time and space that is absolute and objective to the historian. The *incident* is unrepeatable and occurs only once—even though similar actions may occur in different time-and-space settings.[149]

Importantly, Cairns distinguishes the separate use of "history" to refer to *interpretation*. Here, Cairns refers to the subjective interpretation, reconstruction, or restatement of past space-time incidents.[150] The historical *incident* itself is absolute and objective. The historical *interpretation* is a subjective reconstruction of past incidents and their significance.

Cairns is by no means unique in his approach to history. C.S. Lewis writes:

---

148   Bock, "The Words of Jesus," 81.

149   Earle E. Cairns, *God and Man in Time* (Grand Rapids: Baker, 1979), 12-13.

150   Ibid., 14.

> We must remind ourselves that the word *History* has several senses. It may mean the total content of time: past, present, and future. It may mean the content of the past only, but still the total content of the past, the past as it really was in all its teeming riches. . . . [But it also] may mean that portion, and that version, of the matter so discovered which has been worked up by great historical writers.[151]

Finally, Ronald Nash also accounts for this distinction between incident and interpretation. He writes, "The word *history* is ambiguous. It may be used to refer to events that happened in the past or it may mean the narrative, account, or record of the past. That is, history can refer either to that which is studied (the past) or to the study itself."[152]

As these historians demonstrate, any discussion of "history" must carefully distinguish between the past itself and the recording of the past. Only then can a scholar avoid confusion and ambiguity. It is precisely at this point that Bock has erred. He separates himself from historians when he joins the incident and its interpretation together, so that subsequent interpretations affect the meaning of the original event. He does this through an imprecise definition that historians have been careful to shun:

> Though the Gospel writers wrote with a perspective that allowed them to look back on earlier events with a larger context for understanding, they often chose, while looking through that context, to retell the original story with some of the elements of emotional and intellectual ambiguity and uncertainty that the events possessed when they were originally experienced. One Evangelist might choose to cite the remark with its originally perceived ambiguity, while another might bring out its ultimate intended force, a force

---

151   C. S. Lewis, "Historicism," in *God, History, and Historians*, ed. C. T. McIntire (New York: Oxford University Press, 1977), 230.

152   Ronald H. Nash, *Christian Faith and Historical Understanding* (Grand Rapids: Zondervan, 1984), 12.

that became clear in light of subsequent events. Yet both presentations would be accurate to the event's historical thrust. This multitiered nature of historical meaning and portrayal is crucial in appreciating how the Gospels work.[153]

Bock's concepts of multiple meanings should be contrasted, not only with the historians' separation of incident from interpretation, but also with the view of traditional hermeneutics that permits only one meaning to one saying. Milton Terry writes:

A fundamental principle in grammatico-historical exposition is that words and sentences can have but one signification in one and the same connection. The moment we neglect this principle we drift out upon a sea of uncertainty and conjecture.[154]

Bock's intermingling of historical incident with historical interpretation leads to Gospel confusion. He has so merged separate elements that the original event with its original meaning cannot be uncovered. The importance of the historical incident is thus diminished. But as H. H. Rowley has pointed out, the diminishment of the historical underpinnings of the Bible is a deadly mistake:

A religion which is thus rooted and grounded in history cannot ignore history. Hence a historical understanding of the Bible is not a superfluity which can be dispensed with in biblical interpretation, leaving a body of ideas and principles divorced from the process out of which they were born. Nor is the authority of the Bible to be found in the abstract "truth" of a revelation contained in its pages. It lies rather in the totality of the concrete fact and its significance.[155]

153   Bock, "The Words of Jesus," 83-84.

154   Terry, *Biblical Hermeneutics*, 205.

155   H. H. Rowley, "The Relevance of Biblical Interpretation," *Interpreta-*

Bock subjects the Gospels to that danger—even if unwittingly—because he elevates the Gospel writers' interpretation of words and events to a level that clouds the underlying process that gave rise to them. Since he believes in advance that the Gospel writers were "giving the gist" of Jesus' statements, it is not surprising that he believes his scriptural examples demonstrate that phenomenon. But as the subsequent discussion will show, there is nothing *per se* in those passages that compels a conclusion in favor of *ipsissima vox*. Protected from Bock's historical presuppositions, the passages are easily amenable to an explanation that does not lead to an *ipsissima vox* conclusion.

Josephus and Ancient Historiography

The foregoing discussion has noted that *ipsissima vox* proponents assume that the Gospel writers followed Greco-Roman historiographic standards. However, two points need to be made at this juncture. First, *ipsissima vox* proponents offer no evidence to support the assertion that the Gospel writers were familiar with Thucydides. Even if such familiarity is assumed, there is no proof that they patterned their writings after him. The *ipsissima vox* position on ancient historiography is speculation based on demonstrably unproven assumptions.

Second, it is worth noting that the citation of Thucydides proves nothing about the habits of the Gospel writers. Over four centuries separate Thucydides from the Gospel writers. Although there is a verbal parallel to what the *ipsissima vox* writers want to prove, it is a logical leap of cosmic proportions to say (without further proof) that a nearly 500-year-old statement proves what the Gospel writers' standard was when they wrote the Gospel. It would be akin to "proving" modern nautical habits by establishing what Columbus did when he sailed the Atlantic in 1492.[156]

---

tion 1 (January 1947): 8.

156 Wallace concedes, "One of the factors that needs to be addressed is how ancient historiography evolved from Thucydides on" ("An *Apologia*," 4 n. 18). If that evolution is unknown, it is raw, baseless speculation

Is there any historical testimony that would shed light on the regard that the Gospel writers had for Greco-Roman history? Perhaps some clues can be found in the writings of Josephus. It is a reasonable assumption that a first-century Jewish historian would more likely reflect the mindset of the Gospel writers than a fifth-century BC Greek historian. If Josephus is to be believed, Jews did not hold Greek historiography in high regard. Josephus goes into this matter at length, beginning with his defense of Jewish historical accuracy.

> But what is the strongest argument of our exact management in this matter is what I am now going to say, that we have the names of our high priests from father to son set down in our records for the interval of two thousand years. . . . [E]very one is not permitted of his own accord to be a writer, nor is there any disagreement in what is written; they being only prophets that have written the original and earliest accounts of things as they learned them of God himself by inspiration; and others have written what hath happened in their own times, and *that in a very distinct manner also.* [157]

In the quoted section, Josephus argues for a high concern for historical accuracy among Jews, as seen in their careful preservation of the genealogical records of the high priests. Further, he argues that Jews attributed their historical accounts to the direct inspiration of God. The Jews did not emulate the historiography of surrounding cultures, contrary to modern *ipsissima vox* claims. Josephus boasts in the Jewish distinctives:

> For we have not an innumerable multitude of books among us, disagreeing from and contradicting one another, as the Greeks have, but only twenty-two books,

to assert that the Gospel writers followed Thucydides.

157 Josephus *Against Apion* 1.7, in *The Life and Works of Flavius Josephus*, translated by William Whiston (Philadelphia: The John C. Winston Company, 1957), 861.

which contain the records of all the past times; which are justly believed to be divine; and of them five belong to Moses, which contain his laws and the traditions of the origin of mankind till his death . . . and how firmly we have given credit to these books of our own nation is evident by what we do; for during so many ages as have already passed, no one has been so bold as either to add any thing to them, to take any thing from them, or to make any change in them; but it is become natural to all Jews immediately, and from their very birth, to esteem these books to contain Divine doctrines, and to persist in them, and if occasion be, willingly to die for them . . . that they may not be obliged to say one word against our laws and the records that contain them.[158]

Of vital importance to the present subject is the contrast that Josephus draws between these esteemed Jewish historical writings, and the Greek writings that were in circulation:

[None of the Greeks] would undergo the least harm on that account, no, nor in case all the writings that are among them were to be destroyed; for they take them to be such discourses as are framed agreeably to the inclinations of those that write them; and they have justly the same opinion of the ancient writers, since they see some of the present generation bold enough to write about such affairs, wherein they were not present, nor had concern enough to inform themselves about them from those that knew them; examples of which may be had in this late war of ours, where some persons have written histories, and published them, without having been in the places concerned, or having been near them when the actions were done; but these men put a few things together by hearsay, and insolently abuse the world, and call these writings by the name of Histories.[159]

158   Ibid., 1.8, 861-2.
159   Ibid.

Josephus claims that Greek histories had "insolently abused the world" and indicates that they were not worthy to bear the name "histories." Josephus makes it virtually impossible to assert that the Gospel writers modeled their work after their Greek counterparts. The low regard for Greek histories meant that they wrote after a different pattern, a pattern inherited from their fathers. Martin Hengel writes:

> Thus the model for the collection and the literary presentation of the 'biographical' Jesus tradition is [rooted] in the accounts of history to be found in the Old Testament and Judaism, which to a large degree are composed of 'biographical' sections. . . . Josephus shows us that the educated Greek-speaking Jew understood the narrative writings of the Jewish canon as historical works *sui generis,* which differed fundamentally from the works of pagan historians by virtue of their divine authorization and inspiration and were therefore especially reliable. . . . Conscious though they were of the different character of their message, the New Testament historians wanted to take up the tradition which already existed.[160]

Birger Gerhardsson concurs as he describes the Jewish attitude toward the words of their teachers from Old Testament times to Rabbinic Judaism:

> The art of reproducing another person's statements in one's own words, and of abstracting points of view and ideas from someone's words, has been carried to considerable lengths in the Hellenized West. *But the art was not practised* [sic] *in ancient Israel. A person's views were conveyed in his own words.* Authentic statements contained the authority and power of the one who uttered them; this we know from the Old Testament.

160   Martin Hengel, *Acts and the History of Earliest Christianity,* translated by John Bowden (Philadelphia: Fortress Press, 1979), 30-32.

This also applies to Rabbinic Judaism, though certain developments and changes have come about. We can distinguish tendencies towards a more abstract mode of thought. We see above all the method—which was taken to extreme lengths—of subjecting authoritative sayings to thorough penetration and exegesis. *But reverence and care for the* ipsissima verba *of each authority remains unaltered.* In the colleges no attempt was made to give a synopsis of the views of the old masters; their words were quoted— together with the name of the one who had uttered them.[161]

Unless and until they address such fundamental facts, Bock and Wallace should be presumed to be in error, and error of such serious consequence that they threaten the very integrity of the Gospels. The historical tradition that the Gospel writers drew upon came not from the Greco-Roman tradition, but rather from the Jewish/Old Testament tradition that was conscious of the divine inspiration of its writings. The comparison to secular historians that the *ipsissima vox* proponents argue for is invalid, poorly conceived, and lacking evidence—and cannot stand against the testimony of Josephus. The Gospel writers' pattern for transmission of the words of Jesus is not found in ancient Greek historiography, but in the Jewish pattern that paid close attention to the actual words.

Biblical Assessment

The Impact of Inspiration

Not only do *ipsissima vox* proponents fail in their comparison to ancient history, they neglect the *reason* that Thucydides resorted to summaries: he had difficulty remembering the exact substance of the speeches he heard. However, *such*

---

161   Birger Gerhardsson, *Memory and Manuscript: Oral Tradition and Written Transmission in Rabbinic Judaism and Early Christianity, with Tradition and Transmission in Early Christianity,* combined edition with new preface, translated by Eric J. Sharpe (Grand Rapids: Eerdmans, 1998), 130-131 (emphasis added).

memory lapses were not a hindrance to the inspired Gospel writers.
Neither Bock nor Wallace specifically discusses Jesus' words
in John 14:26, which leave no room for doubt on this issue:

> But the Helper, the Holy Spirit, whom the Father will send
> in My name, He will teach you all things, and *bring to your
> remembrance all that I said to you* [emphasis added].[162]

In this verse, Jesus uses the term ὑπομιμνήσκω to describe
the Spirit's work in the lives of the disciples after the resurrection. The term means "to cause one to remember," "put
one in mind," or "remind one of." [163] It is used six other times
in the NT: Luke 22:61, 2 Timothy 2:14, Titus 3:1, 2 Peter 1:12, 3
John 10, and Jude 5. In each verse, the content of the remembrance appears to be something that was previously known
or heard. Here in John 14:26, the remembrance means,
"The Holy Spirit ratifies, confirms and explains the work of
Jesus and thereby brings definitive and conclusive remembrance."[164]

Frederic Godet puts it this way:

> This internal activity of the Spirit will unceasingly recall
> to their memory some former word of Jesus, so that in
> proportion as He shall illuminate them, they will cry out:
> Now, I understand this word of the Master! And this vivid

162 Bock refers only generally to John 14-16 in an obscure endnote
to support the proposition that "Jesus promised that those who passed
on his story would be led into all the truth by the Spirit" ("The Words
of Jesus," 98 n. 25). However, that general comment does not address
the specific language of John 14:26, which is particularly crucial in
distinguishing the ability of the Gospel writers to recall past words with
supernatural clarity. He has glossed over *the* critical biblical text in the
entire discussion. It is difficult to understand why Jesus would promise
help in recalling His words if that promise had no practical effect in the
preservation of His words for future generations.

163 G. Abbott-Smith, *A Manual Greek Lexicon of the New Testament*, 3d
ed. (1991 reprint, Edinburgh: T. & T. Clark, 1937), 462.

164 O. Michel, "μιμνῄσκομαι, κ.τ.λ.," *Theological Dictionary of the New
Testament* (Grand Rapids: Eerdmans, 1967), 4:677.

clearness will cause other words long forgotten to come forth from forgetfulness.[165]

Consequently, the appeal to Thucydides—whatever it may say about secular history—is *irrelevant* to the precision of the Gospels in recording events or the words of Jesus. Thucydides said that he resorted to *ipsissima vox* because he "found it difficult to remember the precise words used in the speeches."[166] Jesus' promise of the direct inspiration of the Holy Spirit meant the Gospel writers would be supernaturally enabled to recall Jesus' words in a manner that freed them from the human limitations of secular historians. As a result, they would not need to resort to *ipsissima vox*. Inspiration placed them infinitely above unregenerate men writing about secular matters.

Yet another consideration makes the comparison between ancient historians and the Gospel writers untenable. Thucydides tells the reader in no uncertain terms that he is not giving exact quotations, but summaries to the best of his abilities. By contrast, the Gospel writers made no such disclaimers. To the contrary, Luke tells Theophilus that he investigated everything carefully "so that you might know the *exact truth* about the things you have been taught" (Luke 1:4 [emphasis added]).

That self-conscious claim to precision, combined with the supernatural ministry of the Holy Spirit, is a telling blow against the historical argument framed to date by supporters of *ipsissima vox*. The pattern of ancient secular history is a false analogy to the ability the Gospel writers had via inspiration and their Jewish heritage.

Once again we see: inspiration matters.

Eyewitness Testimony and Scriptural Accuracy

The prior section has illustrated the phenomenon of accuracy that results from the divine inspiration of Scripture. This next

---

165   Frederic Godet, *Commentary on John's Gospel* (New York: Funk & Wagnalls, 1886; reprint, Grand Rapids: Kregel, 1985), 847.

166   Thucydides 1.22.

section surveys the human perspective of the New Testament writers on their own work. We will see they repeatedly appeal to the reliability of their words due to their position as eyewitnesses to the life and/or resurrection of Christ.

The apostle Peter based his exhortation to elders on the fact that he was a "witness of the sufferings of Christ" (1 Peter 5:1). In another place, he based the reliability of his instruction on the fact that he "did not follow cleverly devised tales when we made known to you the power and coming of our Lord Jesus Christ, but we were eyewitnesses of His majesty" (2 Peter 1:16). Clearly, Peter's status as an eyewitness affected his self-evaluation as a reliable witness to the life of Christ. The church has traditionally believed that Mark drew upon Peter's reliable testimony when he wrote his Gospel.[167]

Elsewhere, the apostle John frequently refers to his position as a personal witness to the life of Christ, as well as Jesus' own affirmation of the apostles' position as reliable witnesses because of their time with Him (John 15:27, 19:35; 1 John 1:1-3; Rev. 1:2). In the passage from 1 John, the apostle covers multiple human senses to demonstrate the reliability of his testimony. His epistle is based on what he has heard, seen, and felt with his own hands. John is also the apostle who recorded Thomas' personal validation of the resurrection (John 20:26-29).

Nor are these apostles alone in their testimony. Paul points not only to his own experiential contact with the Lord, but also that of the apostles and more than 500 other witnesses to the resurrection (1 Cor. 15:3-8).

The theme of reliable eyewitness testimony is also prominent in the book of Acts. After Pentecost, the apostles would be witnesses to the Christ they had personally known (1:8). Personal exposure to the life and resurrection of Christ was a requirement to be an apostle (1:21-22). Peter and Paul validated their sermons with appeals to their status as eyewitnesses of the resurrection (2:32; 3:15; 5:32; 13:31; 26:15). Indeed, the

---

167 See, e.g., Donald Guthrie, *New Testament Introduction*, 4th ed. (Downers Grove: InterVarsity Press, 1990), 82-84.

great power of the apostles' preaching is associated with their direct testimony as witnesses to the resurrection (4:33).

Interestingly, however, the apostolic credibility was based on more than the apostles' status as eyewitnesses to the resurrection. It extended further to seemingly mundane details of Christ's eating and drinking after the resurrection (Acts 10:39-42). Their preaching flowed from their witness of those historical events. Paul notes that his witness for Christ is based on what he has seen *and* heard (Acts 22:15).

These abundant references show that the apostolic community pinned their personal credibility on their status as eyewitnesses who saw, heard, and felt Jesus during His time on earth. This pervasive theme through the apostolic writings can only mean that they were claiming a level of knowledge and precision about the life of Christ that put their assertions and credibility beyond dispute.

Thus, when one looks at the human assertions of the New Testament writers, one finds consistency with the implications of divine inspiration. Not only was God inspiring the words of the writers, He was drawing upon those men who were uniquely equipped to write truth about Christ. Inspiration did not happen in a vacuum—the writers drew upon their personal exposure to Christ and made it a regular part of the compulsion of their preaching.[168] This complements the accuracy to be expected from the doctrine of the inspiration of the Scriptures.

A. A. Trites comments on the importance of the apostles' status as eyewitnesses to the events of the life of Christ. Given the crucial nature of his thoughts, they will be set forth at length here:

> [T]he frequent use of the witness-theme in the NT stresses the importance of the historical foundations of the Christian religion. The principal events of the public

---

168   The apostles' status as eyewitnesses to the life of Christ was part of God's providential preparation of them for the task of writing the Scriptures (cf. Packer, *"Fundamentalism,"* 78).

ministry of Jesus were wrought in the presence of his chosen companions and apostles. They had been present in Jerusalem during the final week, and were in a position to attest the facts of his trial, crucifixion, and burial. Above all, they were competent witnesses to vouch for the fact of his resurrection. . . . In other words, for all the major NT writers the historical facts of Christian origins are of paramount importance. . . . In fine [sic.], it was of supreme significance to the New Testament writers that the apostolic teaching was not based on a collection of myths, but on the experience of eyewitnesses.

In light of the NT's repeated insistence on the role of eyewitnesses and the subsequent stress on the historical nature of the events which the witnesses report, one must raise the question: Has historical scholarship taken this factor sufficiently seriously? Certainly current preoccupation with form criticism, redaction criticism, audience criticism and the like must not blind our eyes to the NT's unmistakable stress on those who were the actual witnesses of the primary events.[169]

The Gospel writers presented a message rooted in the historical facts of Christ's life and the writers' personal participation in His ministry. Thus, "At issue are not doctrines, myths, or speculations, but facts which took place in the clear light of history at a specific time and place, facts which can be established and on which one can rely."[170]

169   A. A. Trites, "Witness, Testimony," in *The New International Dictionary of New Testament Theology*, Vol. 3, ed. Colin Brown (Grand Rapids: Zondervan, 1986), 1047-1048.

170   H. Strathmann, "μάρτυς, μαρτυρέω, μαρτυρία, μαρτύριον," in *Theological Dictionary of the New Testament*, Vol. 4, ed. Gerhard Kittel, translated by Geoffrey W. Bromiley (Grand Rapids: Eerdmans, 1967), 492.

Summary and Conclusions
• •

This chapter has surveyed the historical basis for modern *ipsissima vox* positions. Those positions are based on assumptions about ancient historiography in which secular historians purportedly sought to record only the "gist" of speeches in their writings. Those assumptions were shown to be unacceptable based on historical evidence, and more importantly on the biblical testimony to the inspiration of Scripture and the New Testament writers' status as eyewitnesses to the events and words they recorded.

The *ipsissima vox* views that Bock and Wallace advocate are both historically naïve and theologically unacceptable. Such views insinuate the question, "Did Jesus *really* say that?" Reverant students must reject the very premise and the spirit behind it.

Yes. Jesus said precisely that. The inspired Scriptures tell us so.

5

"Ipsissima Vox" and the Synoptic Gospels

Since Darrell Bock believes in advance that the Gospel writers were mostly summarizing and "giving the gist" of Jesus' statements, it is not surprising that he believes his scriptural examples demonstrate that phenomenon. Bock uses two different kinds of parallel passages in the Synoptic Gospels as evidence of his *ipsissima vox* position: (1) those that differ in their recording of the order of events; and (2) those that are similar but not identical in their detail. These differences between the Synoptic writers, he believes, inexorably lead the interpreter to the conclusion that they were not concerned to preserve the *ipsissima verba* of Jesus—only the substance of what He said. The following analysis is not intended to exegete in detail each of Bock's examples, but simply to show in a broad fashion that the passages can reasonably be understood without resorting to an *ipsissima vox* position.

"Ipsissima Vox" and Parallel Accounts in the Synoptic Gospels

Parallel Events

Bock begins by discussing the parallel accounts of Jesus' temptations in Matthew 4:1-11 and Luke 4:1-13.[171] As is well known, Matthew and Luke reverse the order of the second and third temptations. Since Bock offers that example in the context of his discussion of his position on *ipsissima vox*, he apparently believes that the Gospel writers' arrangement of chronological material somehow proves their willingness to modify the words of Jesus. However, the order of the temptations of Jesus does not contribute to the *ipsissima vox* discussion. There is no logical relationship between an a-chronological arrangement of historically accurate material and the assertion that the Gospel writers did not record the precise words of Jesus.[172] An example that does not involve the words of Jesus is, at best, of only marginal relevance in establishing how the Gospel writers handled His sayings.

Matthew most likely establishes the chronological order with his use of τότε ("then") in 4:5, 10, along with the terminal indicator in 4:10-11 of "Begone, Satan! . . . Then the devil left Him." Luke does not use temporal markers, using καί and δέ instead, which indicates that he did not intend to give a chronological arrangement as Matthew did. Consequently, there is no contradiction between the passages.[173] Neither is there any proof of the *ipsissima vox* position.

A similar analysis applies to Bock's citation of the mir-

---

171   Bock, "The Words of Jesus", 84.

172   Bock indirectly acknowledges this point when he says, "Those differences in order are not an example of error in reporting; rather, they reflect differences in them and emphasis in terms of intended presentation" (ibid.).

173   Bock grudgingly acknowledges the legitimacy of this harmonization ("The Words of Jesus," 97 n. 21).

acle accounts in Matthew 8-9 and its parallels. It is widely acknowledged that Matthew 8-9 is arranged topically rather than chronologically. Bock states, "[These differences] reflect differences in theme and emphasis in terms of intended presentation. They give evidence of conscious choices in ordering events within the Gospel accounts."[174]

Again, however, this ordering of events says nothing about the Gospel writers' treatment of the *words* of Jesus. To arrange material topically rather than chronologically does not mean the author has taken liberty to change spoken words. Broadus speaks for the traditional position regarding the arrangement of material when he writes:

> When we compare the Gospels of Mark and Luke, we find several of these miracles, and the attendant sayings, introduced there in such connections as to show that they did not occur in the precise order in which they are here mentioned. Some of them appear to have taken place before the delivery of the Sermon on the Mount, though during the journey about Galilee . . . and others at various subsequent times in the course of our Lord's labors in Galilee. They are grouped by Matthew without any particular regard to the chronological order, but in such a way as to promote the special design of his historical argument.[175]

Thus, as with the temptations of Jesus, Bock's citation of Matthew 8-9 does not advance the *ipsissima vox* position. There is no necessary correlation between chronological arrangement of genuine, historical material and Bock's assertion that the Gospel writers modified Jesus' words in their effort to summarize His teaching. Arrangement does not negate historical accuracy when the author does not

---

174 Ibid., 85.

175 John A. Broadus, *Commentary on the Gospel of Matthew* (Philadelphia: American Baptist Publication Society, 1886; reprint, *Commentary on Matthew*, Grand Rapids: Kregel, 1990), 58.

imply chronological sequence.[176]

Parallel Sayings

More to the point is Bock's comparison of the accounts of the baptism of Jesus, Peter's confession, and the trials of Jesus, which actually involve the Gospel writers' report of spoken words by Jesus and others. By way of overview, Bock asserts that the differences in the manner in which parallel sayings are recorded *prove* that the writers intended to summarize statements rather than give the equivalent of modern-day quotations. The Gospel writers were content to give the gist of the saying, because otherwise they would have given full and accurate quotations.[177]

By way of contrast, and before examining Bock's specific examples, it should be noted that others have examined the differing statements in parallel accounts and reached an entirely different conclusion. Instead of finding a disregard for verbal precision, these writers find harmonization of the differences in the assumption that each writer recorded different aspects of a broader conversation or discourse.

Benjamin B. Warfield writes:

> It lies in the nature of the case that two accounts of a conversation which agree as to the substance of what was said, but differ slightly in the details reported, are reporting different fragments of the conversation, selected according to the judgment of each writer as the best vehicles of its substance.[178]

Similarly, Kelly Osborne says:

---

176 Robert L. Thomas, "Redaction Criticism," in *The Jesus Crisis*, ed. Robert L. Thomas and F. David Farnell (Grand Rapids: Kregel, 1998), 257.

177 Bock, "The Words of Jesus," 86.

178 Benjamin B. Warfield, "Jesus' Alleged Confession of Sin," *The Princeton Theological Review* 12 (April 1914): 191.

When the words spoken by Jesus are similar but not identical between Luke and Matthew, the assumption should not be that one is more authentic than the other, but that the Lord reiterated the same idea in a similar but not identical manner. . . . This does not provide facile solutions to all difficulties in the text, but it avoids the need to say that one or another evangelist inserted into the text of his gospel words or phrases never actually spoken by Jesus.[179]

Indeed, Scripture itself gives many examples of repeated statements in the same discourse to support this principle. Several examples are found where a statement is repeated *in the same immediate context* for the sake of emphasis. Mark 10:23-24 is one example:

And Jesus, looking around, said to His disciples, *"How hard* it will be for those who are wealthy *to enter the kingdom of God!"* And the disciples were amazed at His words. But Jesus answered again and said to them, "Children, *how hard* it is *to enter the kingdom of God!*

Another example can be adduced from John 14:10-11, where Jesus says, "Do you not believe *that I am in the Father, and the Father is in Me?* The words that I say to you I do not speak on My own initiative, but the Father abiding in Me does His works. Believe Me *that I am in the Father, and the Father in Me."* Paul's comments in Philippians 4:4 also come to mind in this context: *"Rejoice* in the Lord always, again I will say, *rejoice!"*

In light of these examples, one must concur with the writer who said, "Those who so narrowly restrict conversations and discourses to only what is recorded in the gospels apparently have a distorted concept of what communication was like

179   Kelly Osborne, "The Impact of Historical Criticism on Gospel Interpretation: A Test Case," in *The Jesus Crisis,* ed. Robert L. Thomas and F. David Farnell (Grand Rapids: Kregel, 1998), 304.

in these early times."[180] The view of Warfield and Osborne, long held by those who practice traditional harmonization, is not an uncritical failure to deal with problems. Rather, it approaches these issues with common sense and is justified by ready examples from the Scriptures themselves. In the following analysis, that principle will be applied to show that the scriptural evidence does not prove the *ipsissima vox* position. The data is susceptible to better explanations—explanations that Bock usually does not even consider in his article.

The Baptism of Jesus

Bock first refers to the parallel passages on the baptism of Jesus. He notes that the voice from heaven is recorded differently. Mark 1:11 and Luke 3:22 portray the remark as a second person reference made directly to Jesus ("You are my beloved Son"), while Matthew 3:17 records it as a third person remark ("This is my beloved Son"). From this data, Bock concludes that Mark and Luke have probably given the actual remark, while Matthew relays "the general report of its significance."[181] In other words, the Father did not actually say, "This is My beloved Son with whom I am well pleased," as Matthew reports. Instead, Matthew only relayed the general gist of what the Father meant to help his readers understand the significance of the event.

Bock's assessment, however, underestimates the effect that such a change has on the historical accuracy of Matthew's account. Bock's proposal means that Matthew modified the Father's words and changed a private dialogue with the Son into a public affirmation of Jesus. In other words, Bock has Matthew putting words on the lips of the Father that He never actually spoke. The reader of Matthew's Gospel, standing alone, would receive a significantly inaccurate perception of Jesus' baptism. This does not get to the "gist" of the meaning. It alters the dynamic of the entire event.

180   Robert Thomas, "The Rich Young Man in Matthew," *Grace Theological Journal* 3 (Fall 1982): 256.

181   Bock, "The Words of Jesus," 86.

This illustrates the problem with Bock's faulty presupposition of history that merges both the time-and-space incident with the interpretation of that incident. When the interpreter *expects* the Gospel writer to modify statements, it is not surprising when he "finds" what he had predetermined was there. In that process, however, the underlying historicity of the sayings is brought under suspicion. One never knows exactly what was said, because he never knows if the Gospel writer is reporting the actual words that were spoken, or if he is reporting his *interpretation* as though that interpretation were the actual words of the speaker. It casts suspicion on Scripture and turns final authority away from the Word and onto the reader. That is a recipe for long-term spiritual disaster.

In the instance of Jesus' baptism, there are persuasive reasons to believe the Father uttered both the second and third person statements, and the statements can be thus harmonized without doing violence to the context or wording of any of the passages. There is no reason why the Father could not have spoken first to Jesus directly, then for emphasis repeated Matthew's third person version for the benefit of witnesses at the baptism. This approach of traditional harmonization is preferable to an approach that obscures historical clarity and puts non-existent words on the Father's lips.

Peter's Confession

Bock next centers on Peter's confession at Caesarea Philippi (Matt. 16:13-20; Mark 8:27-30; Luke 9:18-21). He sets forth Jesus' initial question as follows:

- Matthew 16:13: "Who do people say the Son of Man is?"
- Mark 8:27: "Who do people say I am?"
- Luke 9:18: "Who do the crowds say I am?"

Bock maintains that the gist of the statement is present, but with variation. He notes the variation between "Son of Man" and the first person personal pronoun "I," along with the difference between "people" and "crowds." He then asks:

Did the translation of remarks in distinct reports of the event merely use two similar Greek words to render one Aramaic one? Or did one writer put the question in language that was more like his own style? Or did one writer simply intend to summarize the event rather than transcribe it? Any of these options is possible. What is crucial to note is that the texts themselves show no necessity to render each other word for word, even in dialogue.[182]

Notice how Bock casts doubt on what Jesus really said. He impugns the reliability of all the writers for the sake of his speculative theory. Bock's analysis does not exhaust the possible alternatives, however. Perhaps each writer gave a *precise*, but not *exhaustive*, account of the conversation. Nothing about these differences *demands* that Jesus was speaking in Aramaic at the time,[183] or that one of the writers made a stylistic variation, or that Jesus' words were paraphrased. The data can be explained equally well by positing an ongoing conversation about Jesus' identity.

Indeed, variations of the same question would heighten the disciples' attention and allow them to focus on Jesus' identity, more so than a single question would. By using repeated questions, Jesus may have been heightening the importance of the moment. He wanted to establish clearly who the people—the crowd—said that He was. Repeated statements of the questions in slightly differing forms would bring that emphasis to the disciples' mind. By establishing the confusion of the multitudes, He set the stage for Peter's great confession that followed.

It would also set the stage for the emphatic question that Jesus addressed to the disciples next: "But who do *you* (ὑμεῖς)

---

182   Ibid., 86-87.

183   While Bock does not allude to it, part of the reason that some believe this dialogue originally took place in Aramaic relates to a possible Aramaic word-play involving Peter's name. For a full discussion and bibliography related to this issue, along with a defense of the position that the dialogue took place in Greek, see Stanley E. Porter, "Did Jesus Ever Teach in Greek?," *Tyndale Bulletin* 44.2 (November 1993): 229-235.

say that I am?" Jesus used repeated questions about the crowds to establish emphasis, and then turned to emphatic vocabulary and grammar in a single question which crystallized the main issue for the disciples and men of all ages: Who *is* this Jesus? The disciples, conscious of the significance of the moment, were about to articulate what the rest of the world was missing. Bock notices the following differences in the account of Peter's reply:

- Matthew 16:16: "You are the Christ, the Son of the living God."
- Mark 8:29: "You are the Christ."
- Luke 9:20: "The Christ of God."

Bock says, "There are two possibilities here. Either Mark and Luke have simplified a much deeper confession as recorded here by Matthew, or Matthew has presented in ambiguous terms the fundamental messianic confession of Mark and Luke."[184] In other words, we have no way to know what was really said.

But again, Bock is guilty of false reduction. An even more plausible alternative exists. Peter, who only recently had been an unsung fisherman, was suddenly in a position to affirm what the multitudes had missed. Jesus was the Messiah! Matthew and Mark both record Peter's use of the emphatic pronoun σύ as he says, "*You* are the Christ." One can almost picture Peter with his index finger pointing at Jesus, and with conviction saying, "I know who You are— you are the Christ, the Christ of God! You are the Son of the living God!"

One further aspect supports this scenario. Peter's confession came at a turning point in Jesus' ministry. As all three Synoptists record, it was immediately after Peter's confession that Jesus began teaching them that he must go to Jerusalem, suffer, be killed, and be raised up on the third day (Matt. 16:21; Mark 8:31; Luke 9:22). Jesus fixed His identity in the disci-

184   Bock, "The Words of Jesus," 87.

ples' minds before He unfolded for them the fulcrum of the redemption of mankind. Godet writes:

> The question addressed to the disciples is designed, first of all, to make them distinctly conscious of the wide difference between the popular opinion and the conviction at which they have themselves arrived; next, to serve as a starting-point for the fresh communication which Jesus is about to make respecting the manner in which the work of the Christ is to be accomplished.[185]

The grammar and surrounding context in this event all call for an emphasis that repeated questions and multiple emphatic responses would supply. Traditional harmonization can well explain the data, preserve the exact words as they are recorded, and at the same time call attention to the high drama of the moment in the life of Jesus. Contrary to Bock's assertion, the choices are not limited to "Either Mark and Luke have simplified a much deeper confession as recorded by Matthew, or Matthew has presented in ambiguous terms the fundamental messianic confession of Mark and Luke."[186] The data is consistent with an entirely different explanation that Bock does not even consider, but that Warfield articulated nearly a century ago—the Gospel writers simply recorded different parts of a larger whole. *Nothing* about the data *compels* the conclusion that Bock suggests.

The Trial of Jesus

Bock's final example relates to different statements made at the trial of Jesus (Matt. 26:57-68; Mark 14:53-65; Luke 22:54-71). Bock sets forth the different questions from the high priest:

---

185   Frederic Godet, *A Commentary on the Gospel of St. Luke* (New York: I. K. Funk, 1881): 263.

186   Bock, "The Words of Jesus," 87.

- Matthew 26:63: I charge you under oath by the living God: Tell us if you are the Christ, the Son of God.
- Mark 14:61: Are you the Christ, the Son of the Blessed One?
- Luke 22:67: If you are the Christ, . . . tell us.

Bock says, "Jesus is asked about his messianic claim, though again the wording differs. So some of the Evangelists must be summarizing."[187] Again, however, the data does not compel his dogmatic conclusion. First, Bock acknowledges that Luke may be describing an event separate from Matthew and Mark. If that is the case (and others would agree),[188] the comparison between the Gospels would be irrelevant to establishing how the Gospel writers reported *the same saying made at the same time*.

Secondly, even for the differences between Matthew and Mark, Bock takes his conclusions far beyond what the evidence warrants. There is no reason why both statements could not have been made: "I charge you under oath by the living God: Tell us if you are the Christ, the Son of God. Are you the Christ, the Son of the Blessed One?" Matthew and Mark would both have exercised verbal precision in quoting only a part of the larger portion of the inquest.[189] It is not at all necessary that one of the writers has put words on the lips of the high priest that he never in fact uttered. Jesus' reply can be handled similarly. "Yes, it is as you say. I am He." A verbally precise account could report a portion of the response without having to give the response in its entirety.[190]

187   Ibid., 88.

188   Robert L. Thomas and Stanley N. Gundry, *A Harmony of the Gospels* (New York: HarperCollins, 1978), 227-30, 329-30.

189   The present writer has experienced first-hand the often-repetitive nature of legal questioning, having participated in hundreds of hours of courtroom and deposition testimony during his former legal practice. Seldom, if ever, are case-determinative questions asked only one time and in one way. A skilled litigator will ask several questions with only the slightest difference in nuance to highlight an issue when he has the opportunity to nail down a point in his favor.

190   R. C. H. Lenski, *The Interpretation of St. Mark's Gospel* (Minneapolis:

After considering all of Bock's examples, it seems that when he is confronted with similar but differing passages, he assumes that, at best, only one statement records the precise words that were actually spoken at the time. Differences are explained by editorial activity by Matthew or Luke.[191] He is drawn to that explanation by his faulty historical presuppositions. The Scriptures he quotes do not prove his position, espe-

---

Augsburg, 1946): 665. Lenski acknowledges this option without committing to it.

191   Grant Osborne reflects the same approach as Bock in his treatment of the parallel accounts of the centurion's cry at the crucifixion. Osborne assesses whether the centurion said that Christ was "the Son of God" (Matt. 27:54, Mark 15:39), or "Certainly this man was innocent" (Luke 23:47). Osborne detects a Lukan paraphrase that does not record the *ipsissima verba* of the centurion (Osborne, "Historical Criticism and the Evangelical," *Journal of the Evangelical Theological Society* 42 [June 1999]: 204). He similarly finds Lukan editorial activity in Luke 11:13 (The Father will give "the Holy Spirit" to those who ask Him) when that verse is compared to Matt. 7:11 (The Father will give "what is good" to those who ask Him). Osborne thus reflects the consistent preference of *ipsissima vox* proponents for finding editorial activity in parallel accounts.

Interestingly, Osborne quotes Paul Feinberg in support of his position ("Historical Criticism and the Evangelical," 202-203, quoting Feinberg, "The Meaning of Inerrancy," in *Inerrancy*, ed. Norman L. Geisler [Grand Rapids: Zondervan, 1980], 301). While Feinberg supports an *ipsissima vox* position in his article, he restricts it to the reproduction of the *identical meaning* of the original saying. Feinberg specifically repudiates Osborne's treatment of Jesus' words in Matthew 28:18 (Grant Osborne, "Redaction Criticism and the Great Commission: A Case Study toward a Biblical Understanding of Inerrancy," *Journal of the Evangelical Theological Society* 19 [Spring 1976]: 83-85) as an improper application of *ipsissima vox* (Feinberg, "The Meaning of Inerrancy," 472 n. 98). Throughout the years, Osborne has struggled to defend his position on the words of Jesus in the Great Commission (Osborne, "The Evangelical and Redaction Criticism: Critique and Methodology," *Journal of the Evangelical Theological Society* 22 [December 1979]: 311; "Historical Criticism and the Evangelical," 206). His latest articulation is, "The Great Commission was Matthew's faithful summary of what Jesus actually said in his resurrection message to the disciples" ("Historical Criticism: A Brief Response to Robert Thomas's 'Other View,'" *Journal of the Evangelical Theological Society* 43 [March 2000]: 115). Osborne apparently intends a distinction between "faithful summary" and "precise quotation," so one following Osborne still cannot declare with confidence what Jesus actually said in Matt. 28:18.

cially when he neglects the possibility that the Gospel writers may have preserved only a portion of a larger conversation or statement.

A Broader View of "Ipsissima Vox"

Presuppositions are crucial to current formulations of the *ipsissima vox* position. Daniel Wallace illustrates this point when he states his views about the Gospels:

> It should be noted that my solution to the synoptic problem embraces Markan priority. This is not the place to defend this view nor is it necessary to do so with the majority of conservative NT scholars. But I mention this so that you know that my starting premise is by no means an unusual one for evangelicals.[192]

Wallace criticizes those who, in his words, let their high view of inspiration influence their interpretation of the text:

> Sometimes we resort to strained and dogmatic interpretations because of a prior commitment to a high bibliology—and it is precisely that theological presupposition that *creates* historical problems for evangelicals; or more sober treatments are less certain both because of the paucity of the data with which we are working and because of a commitment to not allow *our* interpretation of *inspiration* to determine our interpretation of the *text*. Ironically, theological dogma often increases in inverse proportion to the clarity of meaning provided by the text.[193]

192   Daniel B. Wallace, "An *Apologia* for a Broad View of *Ipsissima Vox*," paper presented to the 51st Annual Meeting of the Evangelical Theological Society (Danvers, Mass: November, 1999): 7.

193   Ibid., 13-14 (emphasis in original). The reader will note Wallace's pejorative contrast between those with a high bibliology and "sober treatments" of the text, as if those two items were mutually exclusive. It reflects his own presupposition against allowing the doctrine of inspira-

Wallace argues that the standard descriptions of *ipsissima vox* are inadequate because evangelicals have not considered all the scriptural phenomena that contribute to a full evaluation of the *ipsissima vox* discussion. He asserts these additional phenomena under five categories: (1) Non-dominical sayings where similar words in parallel passages seem to convey a different meaning; (2) The Gospel writers' seeming addition of interpretive comments to the words of Jesus; (3) Differences in speakers in parallel passages of the Gospels; (4) Variations in dominical material that give a different impression of the sense of the original statement; and (5) Seeming dislocation or "patching together" of dominical material.[194] His treatment of this last point is extremely brief and will not be addressed here.

Parallel Passages that Seem to Convey a Different Meaning

Here, Wallace lists several examples that he maintains supports a broad view of *ipsissima vox*. He considers the most significant example to be the parallels in Matthew 12:3-4, Mark 2:25-26, and Luke 6:3-4, in which the Gospel writers quote Jesus' reference to David eating the consecrated bread "in the time of Abiathar the high priest" (Mark 2:26). Mark's account of Jesus' words here creates a historical difficulty. A comparison of the Old Testament passage, 1 Samuel 21:1-7, indicates that in fact, Ahimelech was the high priest at the time of this incident in the life of David. Abiathar did not become high priest until later. Wallace notes that Matthew and Luke do not refer to Abiathar, and suggests their motive in doing so: Abiathar was not the high priest when this incident in David's life occurred.[195]

Wallace believes that Matthew and Luke intentionally omitted the reference to Abiathar because they were aware of the difficulty and therefore sought to remove it from their

tion to inform interpretation.

194 Ibid., 7-8.

195 Ibid., 9-10.

Gospels.[196] He sidesteps the major issues of Christology and inerrancy created by Jesus' words, but asserts that this word change shows "greater hermeneutical latitude than what is envisioned by our normal treatment of *ipsissima vox*."[197]

The approach that Wallace uses by necessity must resort to shaky arguments from silence about the inner motives of Matthew and Luke. This is unhealthy and unsound exegesis. The better approach is to analyze the data that *is* available, and focus on what the author *did* say, rather than guess that Matthew made changes to save the Lord potential embarrassment for His faulty historical recall.

Two points are noteworthy from Wallace's treatment of this passage. First, he refers the reader to three commentaries for a discussion of the issue. Two of those, C. E. B. Cranfield and Vincent Taylor, adopt a historical error by Jesus or Mark as the more likely explanation of the difficulty. The third, William Lane, argues that the reference may be to the section of the biblical book where the reference is found, rather than a chronological reference.[198] Notably absence from Wallace's reading list are conservative treatments that seek to explain the difficulty by affirming that the words came from Jesus' lips without imputing error to Him in the process.[199]

The second noteworthy point of Wallace's treatment is that

196   Ibid.

197   Ibid., 10.

198   C. E. B. Cranfield, *The Gospel According to St. Mark*, in the Cambridge Greek Commentary, ed. C. F. D. Moule (Cambridge: Cambridge University Press, 1983), 116 ("It is perhaps more likely that Jesus himself or possibly Mark mentioned Abiathar . . . forgetting that at the time of the incident he was not yet High Priest"); Vincent Taylor, *The Gospel According to St. Mark* (London: Macmillan, 1955), 217 ("The probability of a primitive error cannot be . . . excluded"); William L. Lane, *The Gospel According to Mark*, in the New International Commentary (Grand Rapids: Eerdmans, 1974), 116 ("Mark may have inserted the reference to Abiathar to indicate the section of the Samuel scroll in which the incident could be located").

199   See, e.g., Joseph Addison Alexander, *Commentary on the Gospel of Mark* (New York: Charles Scribner and Sons, 1864; reprint, Minneapolis: Klock & Klock, 1980), 53-54; D. Edmond Hiebert, *Mark: A Portrait of the Servant* (Chicago: Moody Press, 1974), 78.

his comments about the "hermeneutical latitude" of Matthew and Luke are driven entirely by his presupposition of literary dependence. Only because he assumes that Matthew and Luke copied from Mark does he assert that those two Gospel writers omitted the information about Abiathar, and from that inference, he further infers their motive in doing so: a Gospel cover-up of a glaring mistake by Mark, or worse yet, Jesus. But such a skeptical attitude toward the Gospels is entirely unnecessary.

The interpreter who is committed to the inerrancy of Scripture *does* rule out the possibility of error as a viable option when interpreting a problem passage. And to imply that Matthew and Luke were conscious of Mark's historical error, and edited it out to avoid embarrassment, is to undermine their credibility as trusted historians who knew the facts and represented them faithfully. That line of thinking is contrary to the knowledge that these were men who were devoted disciples of the truth and asserted that they were giving truth (Luke 1:1-4). Instead of promoting confidence in their work, Wallace tempts the reader to wonder what other secrets lurk in the Gospel writers' closets. He promotes skepticism, not confidence, in the inspired record.

If literary independence is assumed, one can explain the omission by the Gospel writers' inherent discretion to select material that advances their cause, and assume that they left out the reference to Abiathar for motives related to their purposes in writing, not to hide historical embarrassment.

On this passage, J. A. Alexander counsels:

> It is best, however, as in all such cases to leave the discrepancy unsolved rather than to solve it by unnatural and forced constructions. A difficulty may admit of explanation, although we may not be able to explain it, and the multitude of cases in which riddles once esteemed insoluble have since been satisfactorily settled, should encourage us to hope for like results in other cases, or to leave what still remains inexplicable undisturbed by efforts at solutions which can only bring discredit on the

Scriptures, or at least on its expounders, without really relieving the particular embarrassment to which they owe their origin.[200]

Interpretive Additions to Jesus' Words

Wallace further alleges that the Gospel writers made deliberate additions to the words of Jesus on occasion with the result that the sense of Jesus' original utterance is altered.[201] To illustrate that assertion, Wallace refers to Luke 5:32, where Luke records Jesus as saying, "I have not come to call the righteous but sinners to repentance." In parallel passages in Mark 2:17 and Matthew 9:13, the quotation simply reads, "I did not come to call the righteous, but sinners," the words "to repentance" not being included.

Again assuming that Luke had Mark's Gospel in front of him as he wrote, Wallace argues that the "special Lukan emphasis" on the theme of repentance suggests that Luke "has actually slightly altered the meaning of Jesus' words here, for that to which sinners are called is neither limited to nor necessarily even qualified *primarily* by repentance."[202] He believes that the Jesus' "original" words (which he asserts did not include "to repentance") focused on the goal of His calling, which was an invitation to the realm of blessing.[203] Wallace maintains that Luke was not wrong to add the phrase, nor that repentance was not implicit in Jesus' utterance. The emphasis merely shifts "a bit" in Luke. He concludes, "However we regard Luke's addition, that it is an *addition* is generally conceded."[204] Again, the *ipsissima vox* position asks, "Did Jesus really say that?"

---

200 Alexander, *A Commentary on Mark*, 54. Alexander suggests as a possible solution that the names Abiathar and Ahimelech were hereditary names in the priestly line, although he acknowledges that there is no direct proof in support of this position.

201 Wallace, "An *Apologia*," 12.

202 Ibid., 10 (emphasis in original).

203 Ibid., 10.

204 Ibid., 11 (emphasis in original).

To whatever extent Luke's addition is "conceded," the concession would seem to postdate the rise of historical criticism. John Broadus affirms that "unto repentance" was actually spoken by Jesus on this occasion,[205] as does Frederic Godet.[206] Wallace's effort to minimize the impact of such a change is shallow and self-serving. The alleged addition involves more than a shift in emphasis; it involves putting words on Jesus' lips that He never spoke and changing the thrust of a key statement about His mission. Under the principles articulated by Warfield and Osborne, it is better to see these differences as one where Luke reported the full version, and Matthew and Mark reported a shorter one.

Change in Speakers

The next example Wallace lists involves places where the Gospel writers seem to attribute the same saying to different speakers. Here, Wallace cites the example of Peter's accusers on the night of Jesus' betrayal. He indicates that "at least two servant-girls, two men, and one group of people each asked the question and got a response. Wallace writes, "But that is *five* questions and *five* denials."[207]

Wallace seems dissatisfied with the suggestion that several people questioned Peter at the same time, because it supposedly does not explain why the Gospel writers focused on different interrogators.[208] Yet it is difficult to see the significance of that concern. It is quite possible (and consistent with human nature) to picture several people standing around Peter. One asks about his association with Christ, and before Peter answers, yet another one speaks and accuses him. Peter's denial in such a circumstance would not constitute two denials, but one denial to variations of the same question. The fact that one Gospel writer attributes one of the questions to one

205 Broadus, *Commentary on Matthew*, 200.

206 Godet, *A Commentary on the Gospel of St. Luke*, 175.

207 Wallace, "An *Apologia*," 13.

208 Ibid.

person, and another writer attributes a slightly different question to another person, does not disregard historical accuracy, as Wallace implies.

Broadus states it well:

> Minute discrepancies as to the exact place and time of the different denials need not surprise us. The accounts are extremely brief, the numerous persons in the court were moving about and much excited, the questions addressed to Peter may in one case or another have been repeated by several persons, and the denial variously made to each of these . . . while yet there were three distinct and separate denials, as indicated in each of the Gospels.[209]

Broadus goes on to state that the Gospel writers "do not undertake in all cases to give the exact words spoken" in support of their view, a statement that reflects an *ipsissima vox* position.[210] Importantly, however, Broadus spoke from the perspective of literary independence, and he believed that independence strengthened the credibility of the Gospel writers' accounts. He urges the reader to compare the testimony of the several witnesses, and be content to notice one or another possible mode of combining the facts.[211] The difference in detail led Broadus to conclude in favor of historical reliability, whereas Wallace writes, "*Perhaps* [there is] a looser treatment of the historical data than we have typically ascribed to the biblical writers."[212]

But there is no reason to doubt the reliability of the Gospels here. It is sufficient for the Gospel writer's purpose to record the question that was asked and attribute it to someone who actually said it. If this is what the biblical writers did when they reported Peter's denials, there is no basis to allege historical inaccuracy. Only those committed to literary dependence must explain why Matthew changed Mark's record of who asked the question. If

209 Broadus, *Commentary on Matthew*, 551.

210 Ibid., 552.

211 Ibid., 553.

212 Wallace, "An *Apologia*," 13 (emphasis in original).

the presupposition of literary dependence is eliminated, and the assumption that the Gospel writers were recording parts of a whole is granted, the matter is resolved.

Thus, while Wallace states that theological presuppositions *create* historical problems for evangelicals,[213] the truth is that historical criticism injects needless complexity into the Gospel accounts. Warfield and Osborne's principle of harmonization—that the Gospel writers were recording parts of a greater whole—is sufficient to address Wallace's concerns in this passage. There is nothing inherent in the data that compels an *ipsissima vox* view—let alone the broad view that Wallace advocates.

Different Impressions

In this brief section, Wallace says that there are places where the Gospel writers give different "impressions" regarding the original scene. (He does not define "impression.") To illustrate, he claims that in the healing of the paralytic, Mark 2:4 implies that a mud thatch roof was torn apart to gain access to Jesus, while Luke 5:19 calls it a tiled roof. After discussing some alternative resolutions of this difference and finding them unlikely, Wallace follows Robert Stein, who says "Luke here 'contextualized' the tradition for Theophilus and provided a thought-for-thought translation, whereas Mark in his description provided a word-for-word translation."[214]

That explanation is unsatisfactory. It means that Luke referred to "mud" as "tile," which is historically inaccurate and inconsistent with Luke's purpose to convey to Theophilus "the exact truth." Not only that, but Wallace's proposed solution hardly qualifies even as a thought-for-thought translation.

Is there a plausible explanation that would account for the different terms in Mark and Luke? D. Edmond Hiebert thinks so. He describes a roof consisting of beams that were covered

213   Ibid. (emphasis in original).

214   Robert L. Stein, *Luke* in the New American Commentary (Nashville: Broadman Press, 1992), 176.

with stone slabs or plates of burnt clay. On top of those tiles was a coat of clay spread about and rolled hard to keep out the rain. The paralytic's friends would have dug out the top layer of clay, and once they had a large enough hole, they would have lifted the underlying tiles to make the opening.[215] Once again, an alternative explanation, not considered by the historical critic, is found that adequately deals with all the data without impugning the accuracy or authority of the text.

Summary and Conclusions

This chapter has examined the scriptural examples used by *ipsissima vox* proponents in support of their position. While many examples are set forth, it is clear than traditional harmonization can resolve the seeming discrepancies without straining the data.

215   Hiebert, *Mark*, 63.

6

Review and Conclusions

In Chapter 1, this book introduced the current status of evangelical scholarship on the *ipsissima vox* issue. The research showed that many evangelicals have embraced a view of *ipsissima vox* that allows for editorial modifications to the words of Jesus, even when that results in a change of meaning from His original utterance. Proponents argue that the modern reader should *expect* to find predominately *ipsissima vox* in the Gospels instead of the *ipsissima verba*. Whether that view is consistent with the evangelical doctrine of inspiration and inerrancy was raised.

Beginning in Chapter 2, the book examined the doctrine of verbal inspiration and its implications for the biblical interpreter. It was shown that inspiration requires a deductive approach to the Scriptures, one that assumes in advance that the Bible is true in all that it affirms. Such an approach prevents the interpreter from concluding that the Bible is in error on any point.

Another implication of verbal inspiration is that the interpreter should expect to find verbal precision in the Scriptures. Under the influence of the Holy Spirit, the biblical writers chose precisely the words God desired as they penned the Holy Writ. This principle was demonstrated in the prophetic, historical, and grammatical details of the Scriptures. Minute details are shown to be accurate, showing the reliability of Scripture and also the attention to detail that the biblical authors used.

Chapter 2 further showed that not all evangelicals allow inspiration to influence their interpretation of biblical data, particularly as historical issues are being addressed. These writers conduct their analysis first by presumed standards of historical inquiry, so as not to let any theological bias color their interpretation. This view was evaluated and shown to be fundamentally flawed, because Scripture is above the standards of historical inquiry, not subject to them.

Chapter 3 evaluated the impact of genre analysis on the interpretation of the Gospels. It was shown that many scholars argue that genre analysis is indispensable for a proper interpretation of the Gospels. The various definitions of "genre" were analyzed, along with several proposals for the genre classification of the Gospels. Genre critics conduct this analysis because they believe genre is an indispensable hermeneutical key to interpretation.

An evaluation of genre analysis, however, found it lacking in several respects. To date, writers do not even agree on a definition of "genre." Further, it was shown that there is widespread disagreement on the classification of the genre of the Gospels among genre critics. Even beyond those disagreements, there are numerous reasons to believe the Gospels are a unique kind of literature, given their anonymity, language, and style. Thus, the role of genre in the interpretation of the Gospels was brought into serious question. It was concluded that, given its numerous weaknesses, genre classification should not be allowed to override the clear meaning or historical affirmations of the text.

Chapter 4 examined the use of ancient secular historiography to establish the standard of verbal precision to expect from the Gospels as they record the words of Jesus. *Ipsissima vox* proponents argue that the ancient historians only sought to record the gist of a statement, not the precise words. From that statement, they argue that the Gospel writers used that standard as the prevailing historiographic method of the day. This encourages the modern reader to expect *ipsissima vox* as he studies the Gospels. An examination of the writings of Darrell Bock and Daniel Wallace showed that evangelicals differ on the amount of latitude which the Gospel writers would have employed in recording the words of Jesus.

After stating those views, the parallel between ancient history and the Gospels was assessed. It was found that Darrell Bock's view overestimates the commitment to accuracy of secular historians at the time of Jesus, because secular historical writings had given greater prominence to rhetorical flourishes over verbal precision. Thus, secular speeches are of questionable reliability to even give the gist of the saying. Still further, even a conservative view of ancient history allows for an admixture of truth and error in secular writings. To adopt that standard as the prevailing standard for the Gospel writers is to invite the conclusion that the Scriptures contain error. This would clearly violate the doctrine of inspiration.

Yet another difficulty with modern *ipsissima vox* writings is that they fail to give due weight to the pattern of Jewish historiography. Jewish writers had disdain for Greek histories and greater interest in preserving the words of their teachers. The Gospel writers would have drawn upon the Jewish pattern, and thus would have been highly unlikely to pattern their writings after the Greeks. The more precise Jewish standard would have prevailed.

Another telling blow against current *ipsissima vox* writings is their failure to deal with John 14:26, which promises the disciples the help of the Holy Spirit to recall the words of Jesus. This supernatural memory assistance placed the Gospel writers in a category of their own in being able to recall the words of Jesus as they wrote the Gospels. There would have been no human memory limitations that required them to resort to an *ipsissima vox* approach to Jesus' words. That, combined with the unique role of eyewitnesses in the composition of the Gospels, leads the reader to expect a much higher degree of precision than is currently allowed by *ipsissima vox* writers.

Chapter 5 examined the scriptural support of the *ipsissima vox* position, evaluating both parallel events and parallel sayings. It was shown that evangelical *ipsissima vox* writers have not even *attempted* to employ traditional harmonization to resolve the differences, even though the differences can be resolved without resorting to an *ipsissima vox* position.

This book has established the current statements on *ipsissima vox* are inconsistent with an orthodox view of the inspiration of Scripture. Despite the traditional insistence on the value of every word of revelation, and the interpretive principle that a change in word results in a change of meaning, *ipsissima vox* proponents assert that the Gospel writers changed the words of Jesus or made them up to suit their purposes.

In assessing the results of this research, I would offer the following observations. As it is currently framed, the evangelical *ipsissima vox* discussion undermines a high view of Scripture. The comparison with ancient historiography is especially troublesome, since even the most conservative view of ancient history concedes that it allows room for substantial error in the recording of speeches. These evangelicals create a trap in which they (or their students) will impute error to the Gospels as well.

The potential remedy for this defect is closer examination of the Jewish pattern of historiography and an assessment of how that would affect whether any level of *ipsissima vox* would have been acceptable to a first-century, predominately Jewish audience. As for now, the disregard for the higher standards of precision in Jewish historiography renders current treatments of the *ipsissima vox* issue useless for the devout interpreter.

Similarly, the current bias against traditional harmonization has undermined the approach of evangelical *ipsissima vox* writers. Good research technique calls for a fair examination of all viable explanations of the data at hand. As shown in this book, *ipsissima vox* writers not only choose against fair harmonizations, they most often do not even consider them. This vitiates their claim of having offered the most plausible explanation of the data.

This book does not claim to have established an *ipsissima verba* view of the Gospels. While an *ipsissima verba* has been assumed in the explanation of parallel accounts of the sayings of Jesus, the research detailed in this book does not address the matters necessary to sustain an *ipsissima verba* conclusion.

Similarly, this book does not suggest that the results of this research forever rule out an *ipsissima vox* view. An acceptable presentation of *ipsissima vox*, however, will need to contend with the issues of inspiration and inerrancy raised here.

7

2023 Epilogue

Many years ago—more than I care to count—I was a new believer. Those who were helping me to grow in my newborn faith introduced me to the discipline of *word-perfect* Scripture memorization. Precise work on the front end enabled accurate recall on the back end, when Scripture was needed at a moment's notice for the sake of discernment, encouragement, or evangelism. Those dear saints were right about the long-term effect. I owe a great deal to them for that contribution to my sanctification.

Old Testament writers expressed the same reverence for these precious words.

> I have not departed from the command of His lips; I have treasured the words of His mouth more than my necessary food (Job 23:12).

> Your words were found and I ate them, and Your words became for me a joy and the delight of my heart; for I have been called by Your name, O LORD God of hosts (Jer. 15:16).

Whatever their private reverence may be, modern *ipsissima vox* proponents emphatically do not lead their disciples to a proper regard for the written Word of God. Based on flimsy historical evidence and flabby scholarly argument, they toss the words of Jesus into the wastebasket as if they were so many table scraps, to be easily disposed and forgotten.

But their approach is contrary to the entire tenor of Scripture and the reality of human nature. Consider what Scripture says about the Word (and words) of Christ. Surely any doctrine about the recording of Jesus' words should begin with the Gospels' own teaching about His words. Grasp the tenor of the following samples:

> Man shall not live on bread alone, but on every word that proceeds out of the mouth of God (Matt. 4:4).

> The multitudes were amazed at His teaching; for He was teaching them as one having authority, and not as their scribes (Matt. 7:28-39).

> All the people were hanging upon His words (Luke 19:48).

> Never did a man speak the way this man speaks (John 7:46).

> Heaven and earth shall pass away, but My words shall not pass away (Matt. 24:35; cf. Mark 13:31; Luke 21:33).

> Jesus the Nazarene . . . was a prophet mighty in deed and word in the sight of God and all the people" (Luke 24:19).

> Were not our hearts burning within us while He was speaking to us on the road, while He was explaining the Scriptures to us? (Luke 24:32).

> The words that I have spoken to you are spirit and are life (John 6:63).

If you abide in My word, then you are truly disciples of Mine" (John 8:31).

He who does not love Me does not keep My words; and the word which you hear is not Mine, but the Father's who sent Me (John 14:24).

If you abide in Me, and My words abide in you, ask whatever you wish, and it shall be done for you (John 15:7).

The words which You gave Me I have given to them (John 17:8).

He who rejects Me, and does not receive My sayings, has one who judges him; the word I spoke is what will judge him at the last day. . . . The Father Himself who sent Me has given Me commandment, what to say, and what to speak. Therefore the things I speak, I speak just as the Father has told Me (John 12:48-50).

So faith comes from hearing, and hearing by the word of Christ (Rom. 10:17).

In light of such passages, it is small wonder that when their faith was challenged, the disciples responded, "Lord, to whom shall we go? You have *words* of eternal life" (John 6:68; emphasis added). They focused on His *words* as the reason they could never depart. These magnificent *words* came from the Father, burned in the hearts of those who heard them, and have an eternal significance that will last beyond the present heavens and earth.

According to the *ipsissima vox* proponents, we are to believe not only that the disciples took substantial editorial liberty to substitute their words for those of their Master, but also that those who heard the words allowed them to be changed without objection. That is utterly contrary to human nature and the love those devoted first-century disciples had for Christ. Would not someone, somewhere, stand up and demand precision in the accounting of the words of *God* in human flesh? Would not someone, somewhere, say, "That's close, but here is precisely what He said?"

Robert Stein—a staunch proponent of the *ipsissima vox* position—says that modern scholar Joachim Jeremias considered the recovery of the *ipsissima verba* so important that he made it the goal of his lifetime study.[216] If Jeremiah Joaichim could be so passionate as to spend his life recovering the *ipsissima verba* of Jesus 2000 years later (whatever we may think of his methods), are we to believe that the inspired writers of Scripture would be less motivated to do the same? Would the humble eyewitnesses of the *resurrection*—who were uniquely commissioned as the custodians of his appearance—approach their duty with such a casual attitude to substitute their words for those of the Master (cf. Luke 1:1-4; 1 John 1:1-3)?

Think of it this way. These self-same scholars labor with editors to make sure their publications are verbally precise. They would object vociferously if a student deliberately changed the meaning of their teaching in a written article, and they would perhaps subject the student to academic discipline. And yet we are to believe these men when they promote a theory of Scripture that subject the words of Jesus to a scholarly game of badminton, batted back and forth with tentative suggestions and conclusions, with no real authority attached to the *actual words His apostles initially heard, and then remembered and recorded under the inspiration of the Holy Spirit?* As John Wenham says:

> The idea that [the early church] had little concern to preserve an accurate account of the words and deeds of Jesus is highly improbable. In Judaism oral material was learnt verbatim and passed on verbatim as 'holy tradition.'[217]

216   Stein, *The Synoptic Problem*, 156.

217   Wenham, *Christ and the Bible*, 3d ed., 46.

If God-given words are promised for the emergencies of persecution, how much more might they be expected for her abiding Scripture. If remembrance of the Lord's words was necessary for the proper instruction of the infant church when many eyewitnesses were still alive, how much more when they were dead. It would be most natural to believe that the promises of remembrance and of guidance into new truth found their most far-reaching fulfillment in a New Testament Canon.[218]

The nature of Scripture was determined by the inspiration of the Holy Spirit, who is the God of truth, not by secular writers who had no part with the people of God.

Dear reader, when you hold the Bible, you hold a trustworthy account of the words, deeds, and promises of Jesus Christ. Beware of the arguments of learned but misguided men who condition you at every turn to wonder, "Did Jesus really say that?" God has given to us what He wants us to have in the Word, and warns us all against tampering with the end product the Spirit produced:

> I testify to everyone who hears the words of the prophecy of this book: if anyone adds to them, God will add to him the plagues which are written in this book; and if anyone takes away from the words of the book of this prophecy, God will take away his part from the tree of life and from the holy city, which are written in this book.
> (Rev. 22:18-19)

Sola Scriptura

---

218   Ibid., 117.

THE TRUTH PULPIT

Teaching God's People God's Word

To learn more about Don Green and his Bible-teaching resources, visit thetruthpulpit.com. You can subscribe to podcasts of his full-length messages from Truth Community Church, the daily "The Truth Pulpit" audio program, and his weekly feature "Through the Psalms."

Also by Don Green

The Bible tells us to expect difficult trials as part of the Christian life. You know that you should trust God when hard times come, but exactly how do you trust God when life seems to fall apart at the seams? This life-changing study from the book of Habakkuk will teach you how to move from trials to spiritual triumph—even if your circumstances do not change.

"No matter who you are or where you are in life, I know you will benefit greatly from Pastor Green's insights on the prophecy of Habakkuk and the problem of human misery."
— John MacArthur: from *The Foreword*

". . . blessings overflow in encouragement and comfort for all who will read it and take its counsel to heart."
—Tom Ascol: Pastor, Grace Baptist Church of Cape Coral, FL; President of Founders Ministries and The Institute of Public Theology

Trusting God in Trying Times: Studies in the Book of Habakkuk
Hardcover, 128pp
ISBN 978-0-9987156-1-2
www.ttwpress.com

Also by Don Green

John MacArthur began his ministry at Grace Community Church in Sun Valley, California in 1969. Since then, millions have known him as a steadfast voice for biblical authority and teaching. But what kind of man is he in private? Don Green observed him closely over a fifteen-year period in leadership roles at Grace Church and Grace to You. *In John MacArthur: An Insider's Tribute*, you'll find winsome vignettes, exclusive interviews, and never-before-published photos to give you access to the man whose service to Christ has benefitted so many—all as a testimony to the grace of God in the life of John MacArthur.

John MacArthur: An Insider's Tribute
Deluxe Coffee-Table Quality Hardback, Color Throughout, 80pp
ISBN 978–0–9987156–0–5
www.ttwpress.com

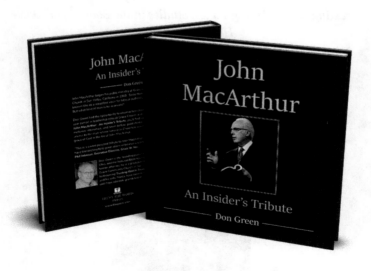

Printed in the USA
CPSIA information can be obtained
at www.ICGtesting.com
LVHW011730300124
770175LV00004B/446